101
WAYS TO USE A
UNICORN

Robb Pearlman

Illustrations by Dave Urban

UNIVERSE

#1: Popsicle Holder

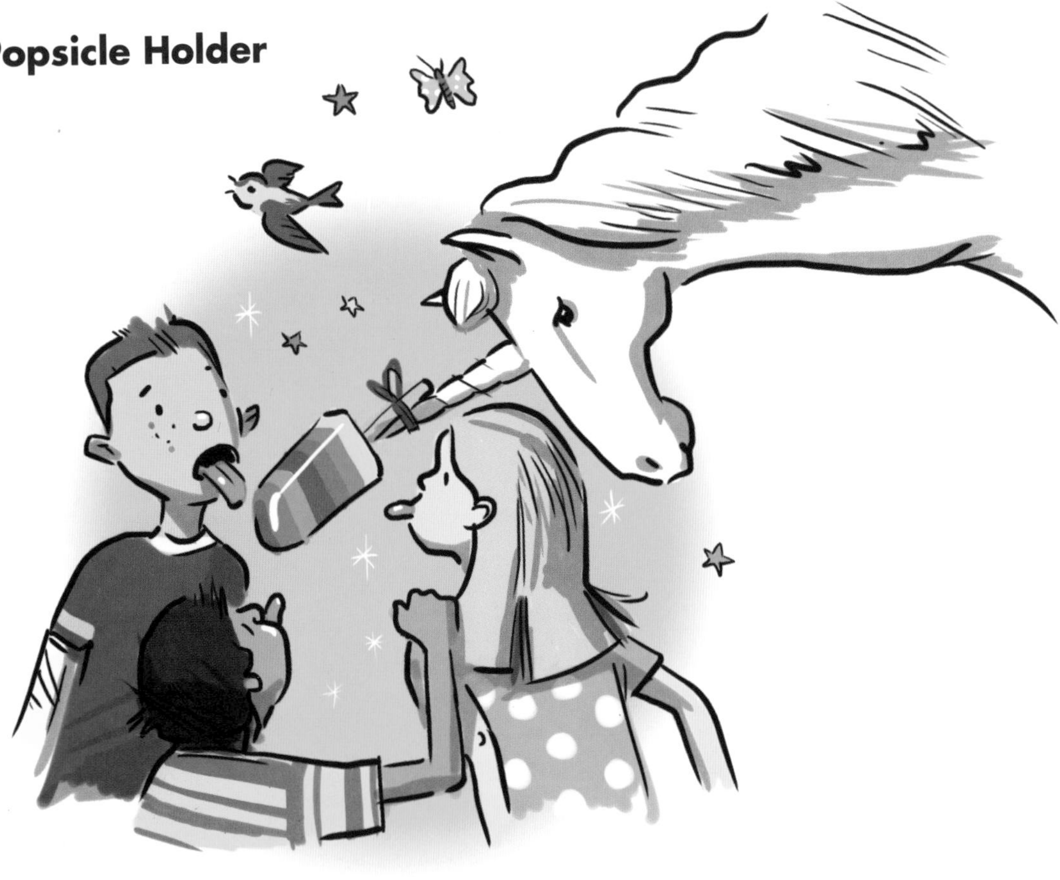

#2: Locksmith

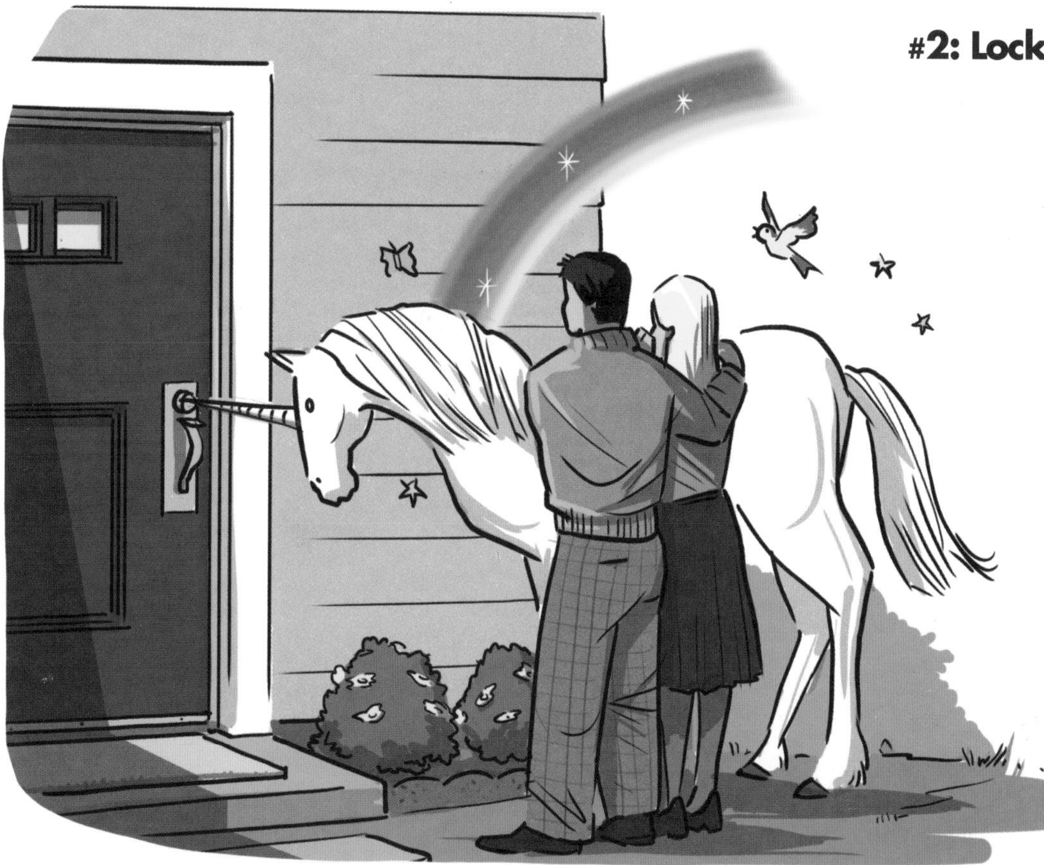

#3: Tent Pole

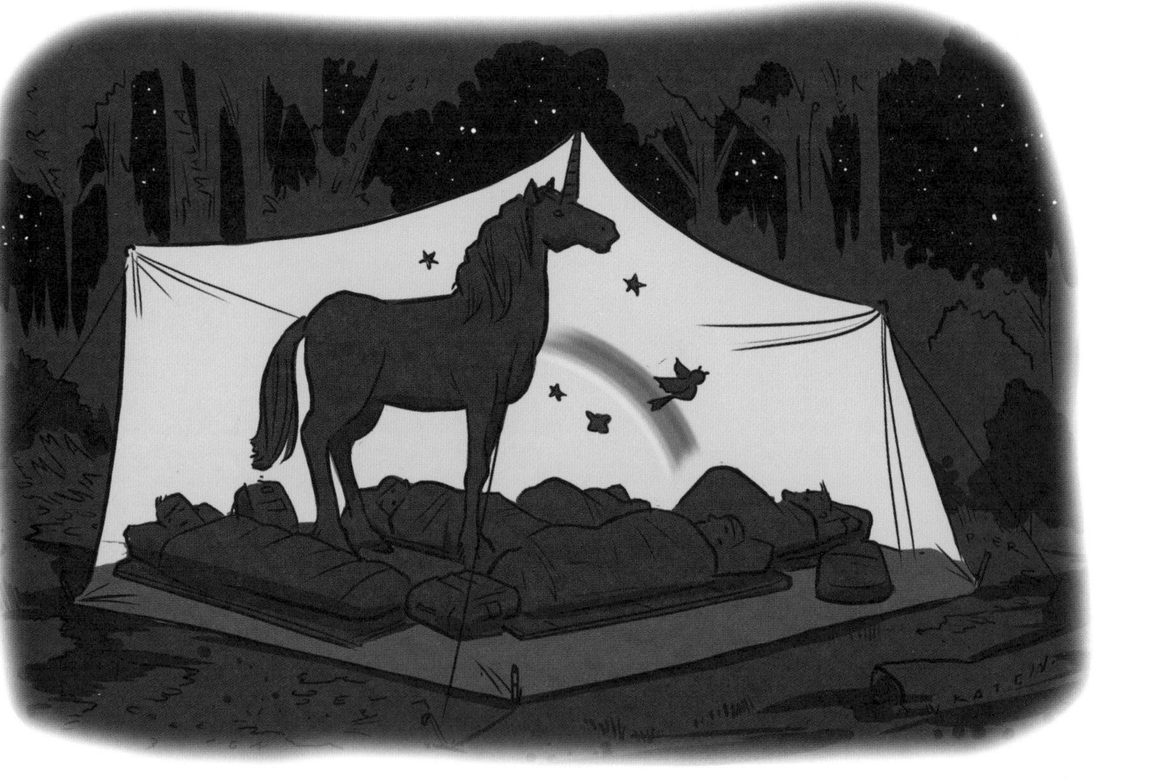

#4: Lamp

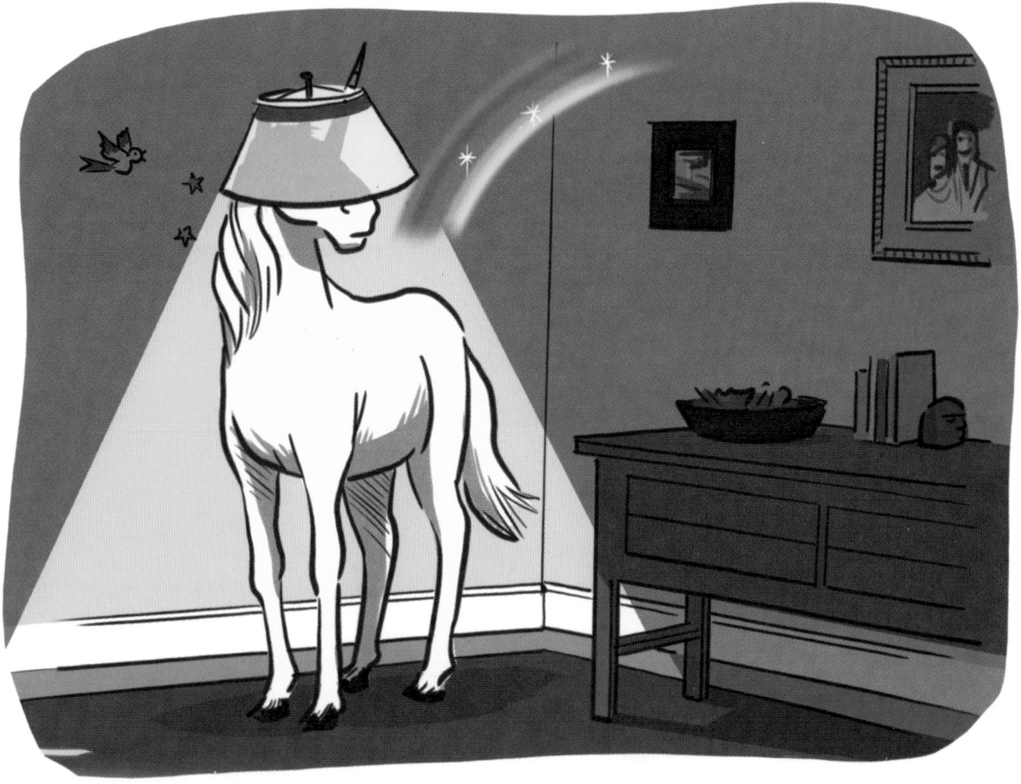

#5: Proctologic Instrument

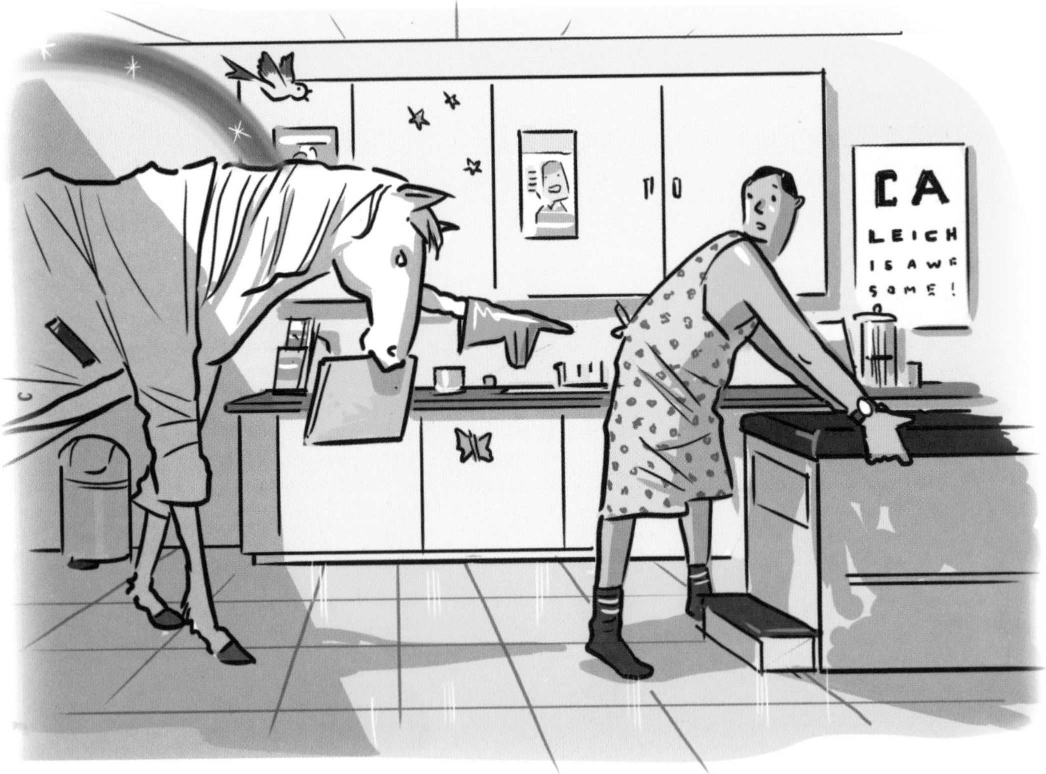
CA
LEICH
IS AWE
SOME!

#6: Paperweight

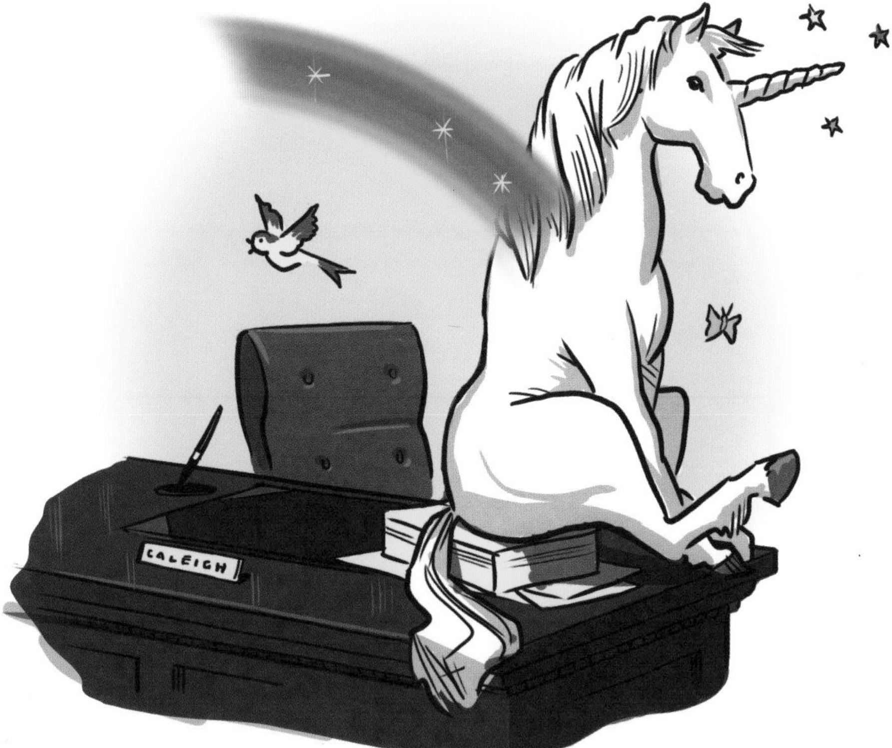

CALEIGH

#7: Lady's Maid

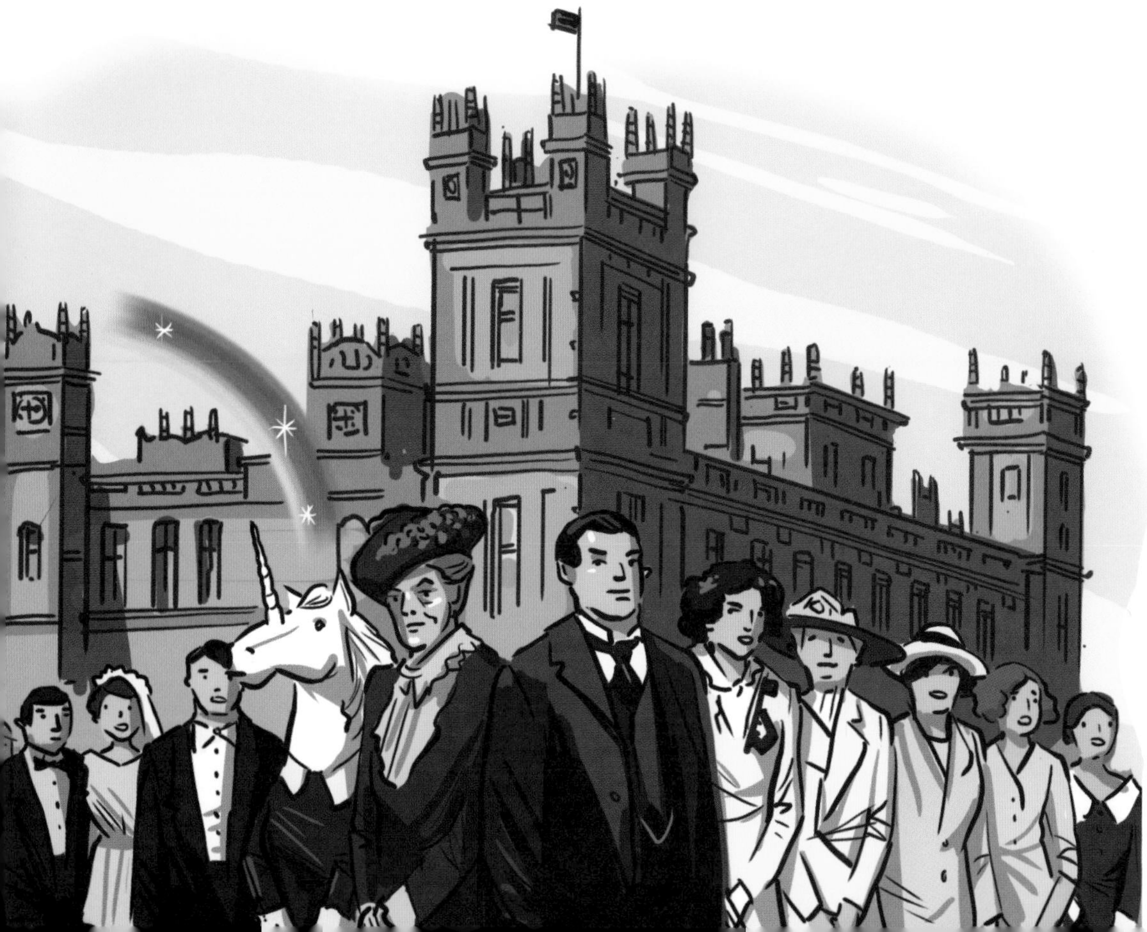

#8: Siren

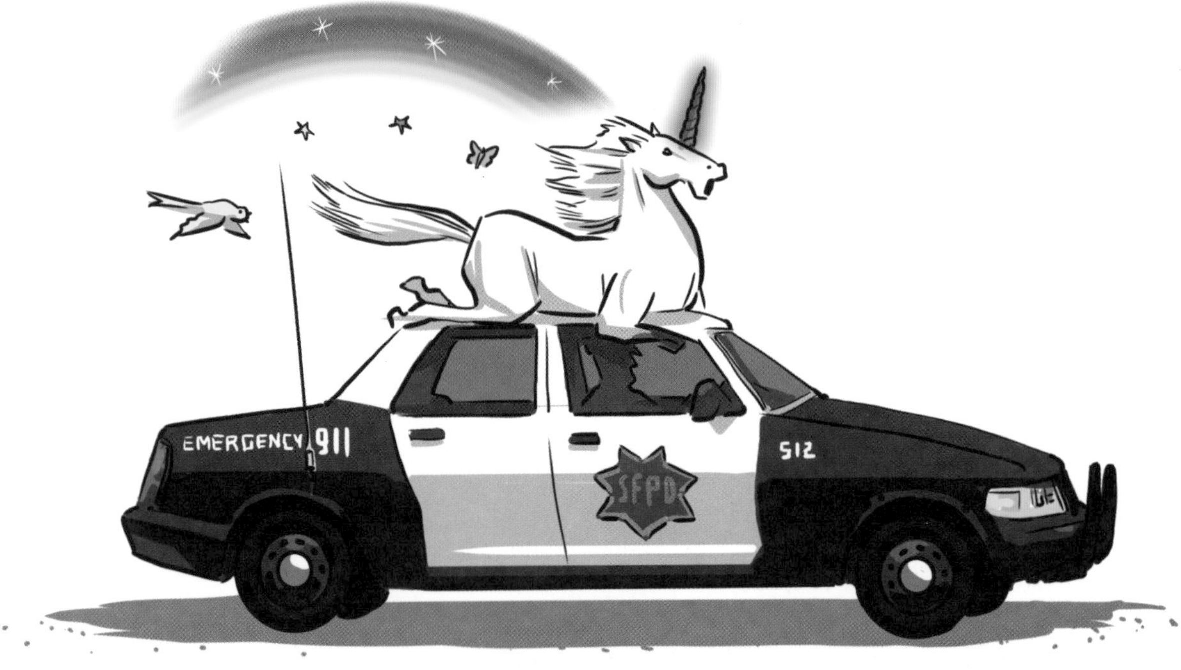
EMERGENCY 911
512
SFPD

#9: Siren

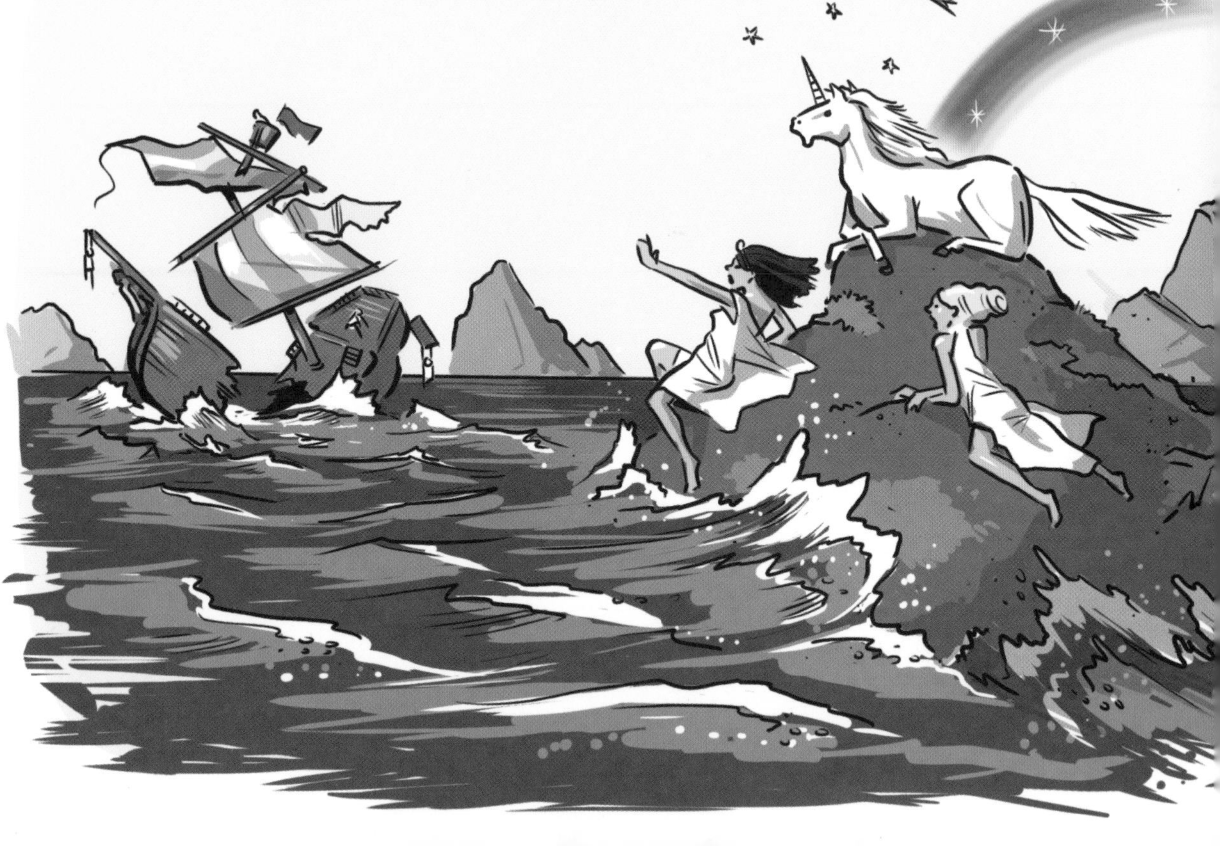

#10: Plow

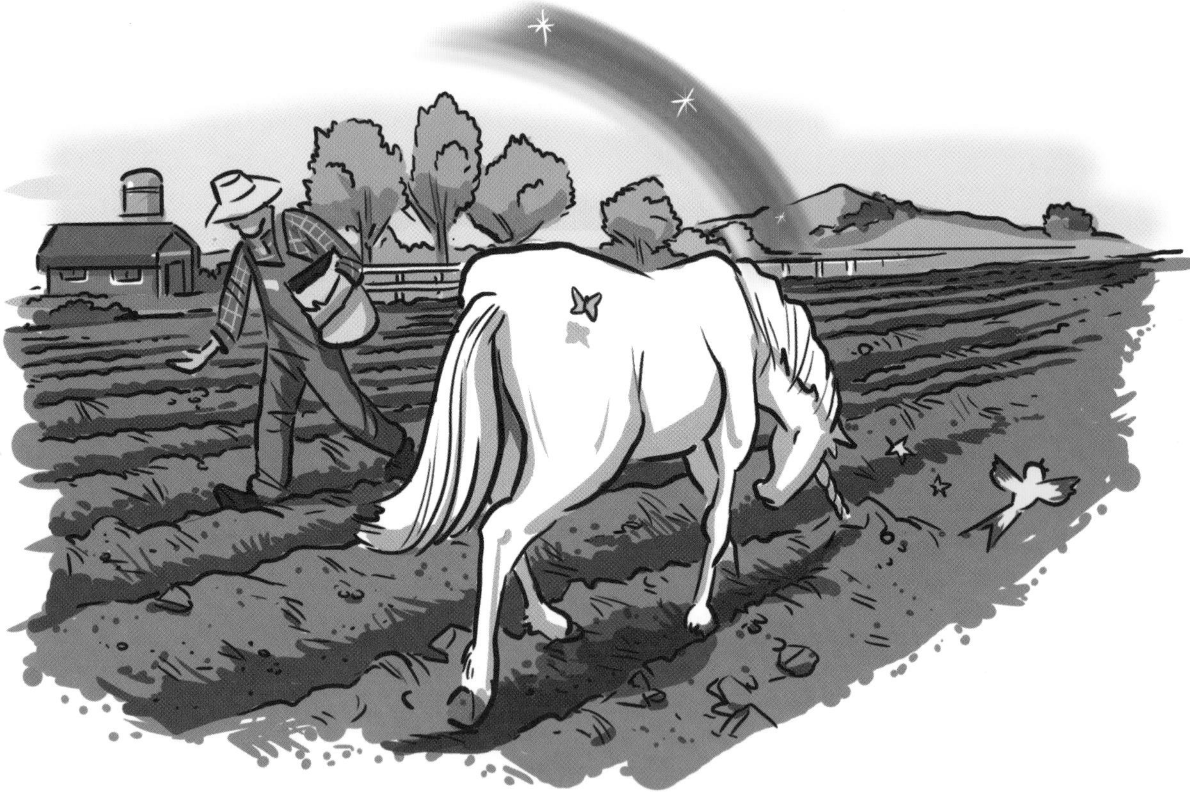

#11: Greek Diner Check Spindle

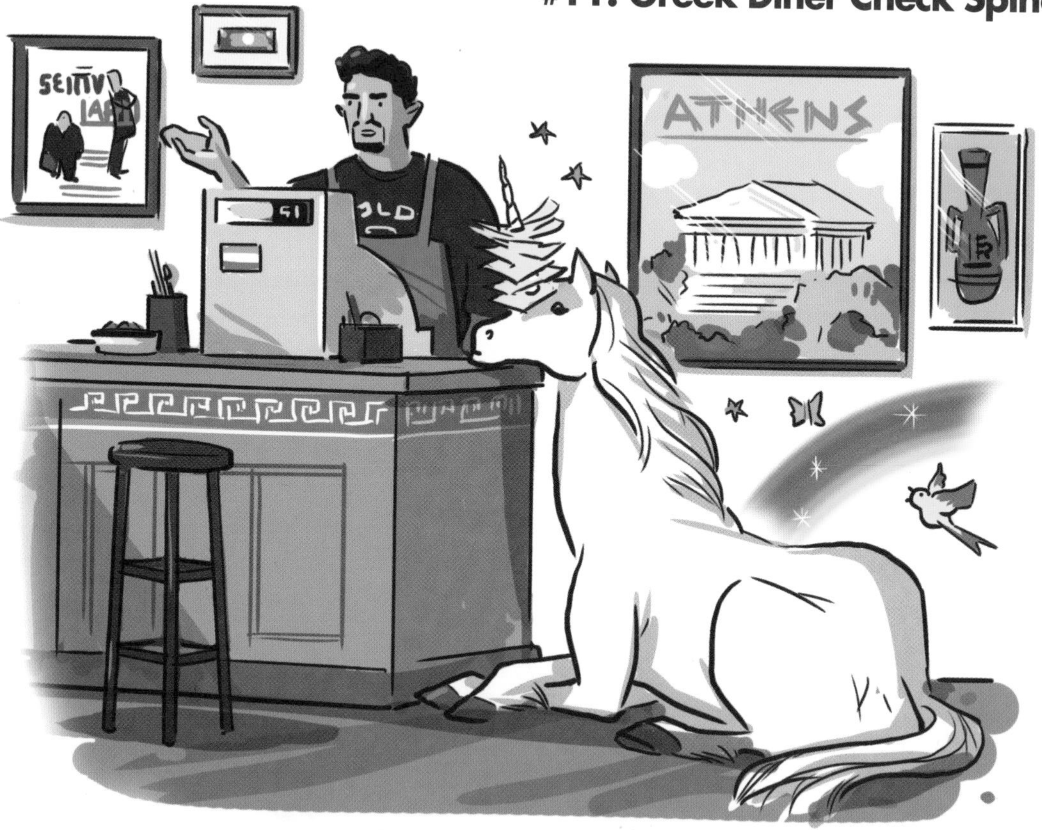
ATHENS

#12: Mic Stand

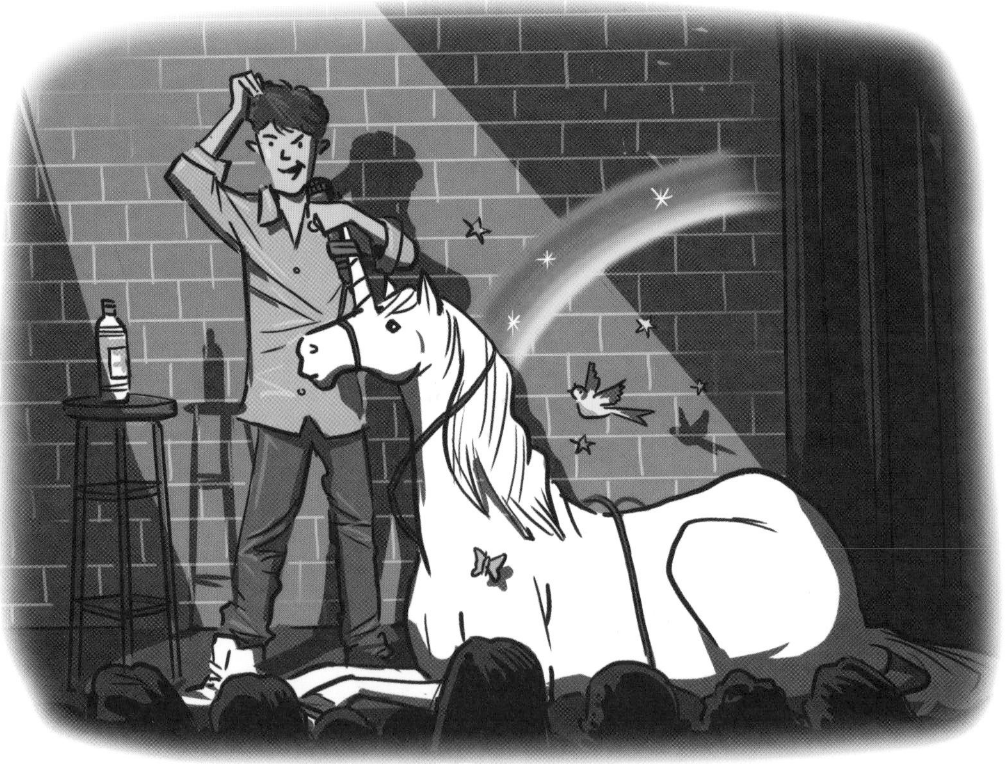

#13: Bookmark

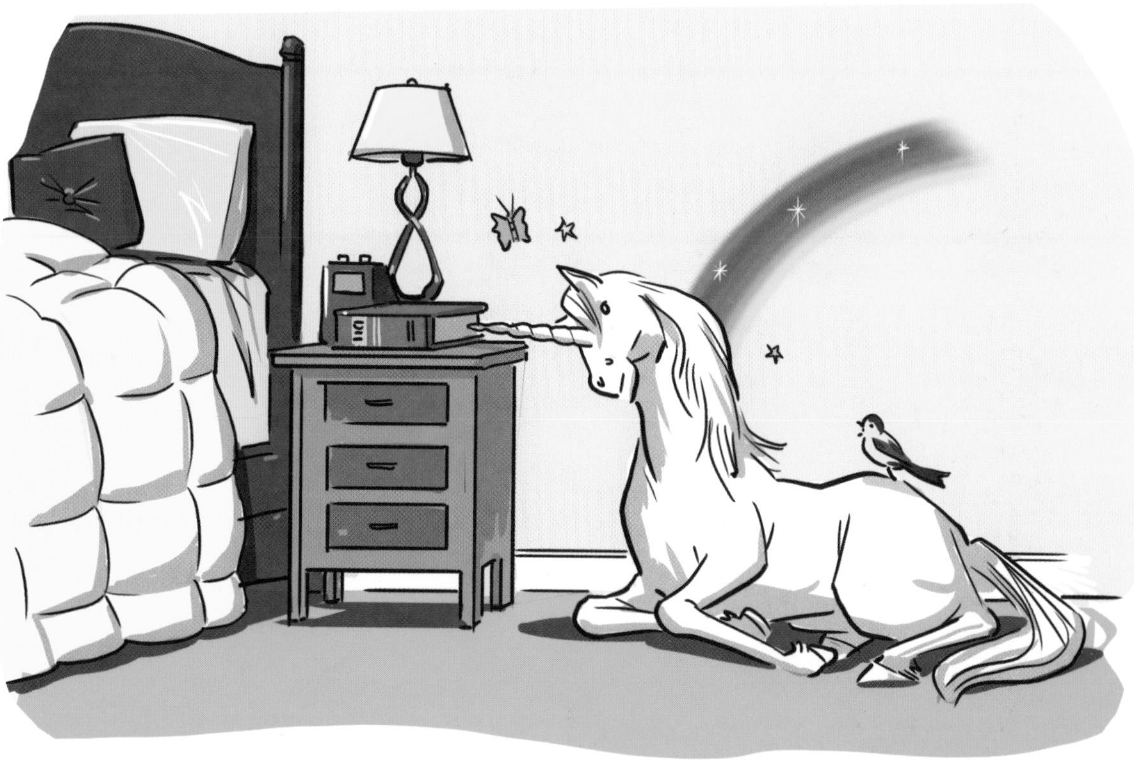

#14: Spotter

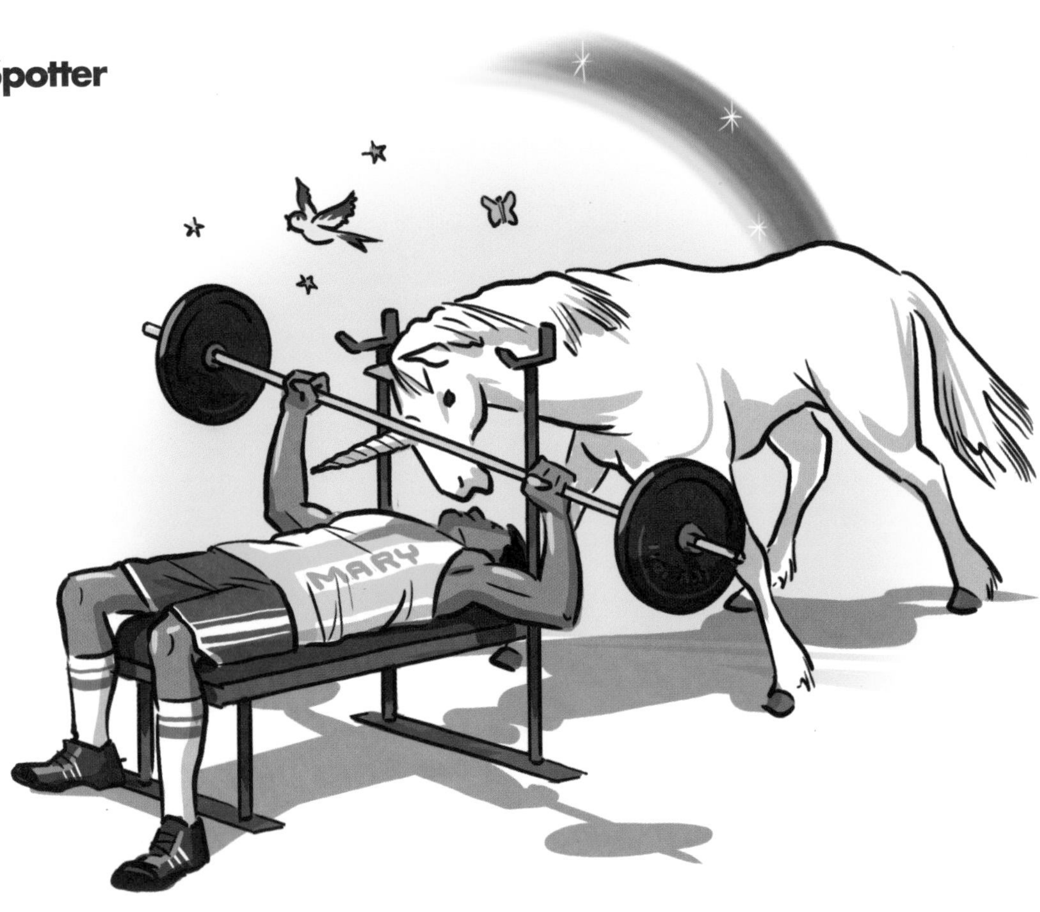
MARY

#16: Cougar Bait

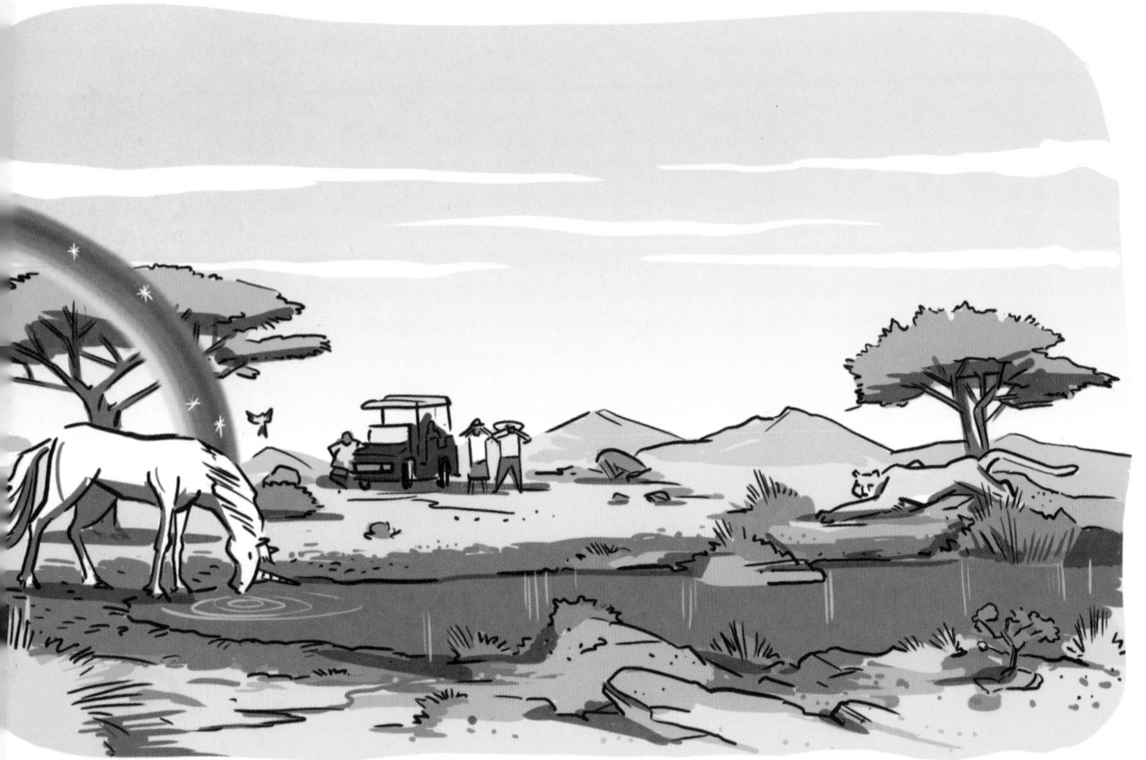

#15: W

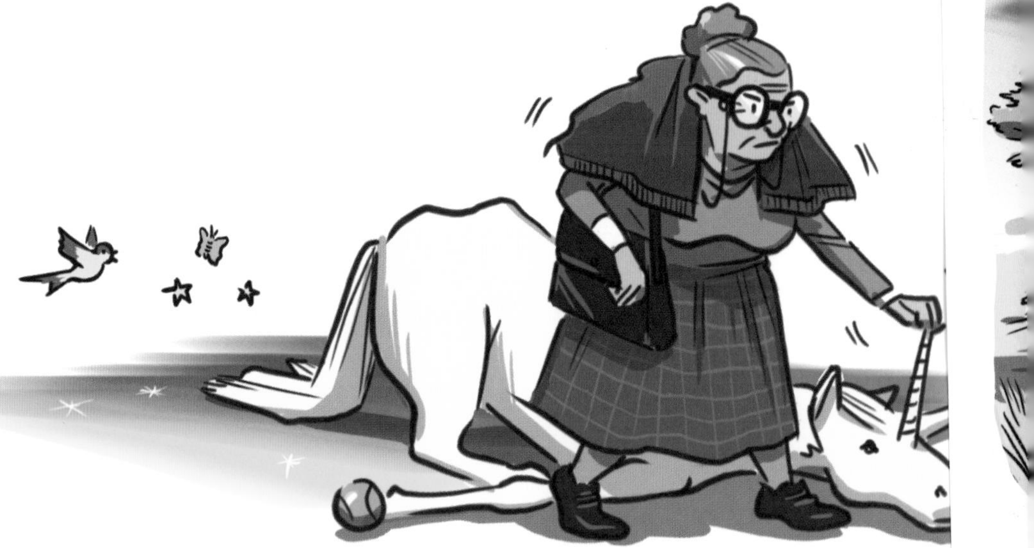

#17: Cougar Bait

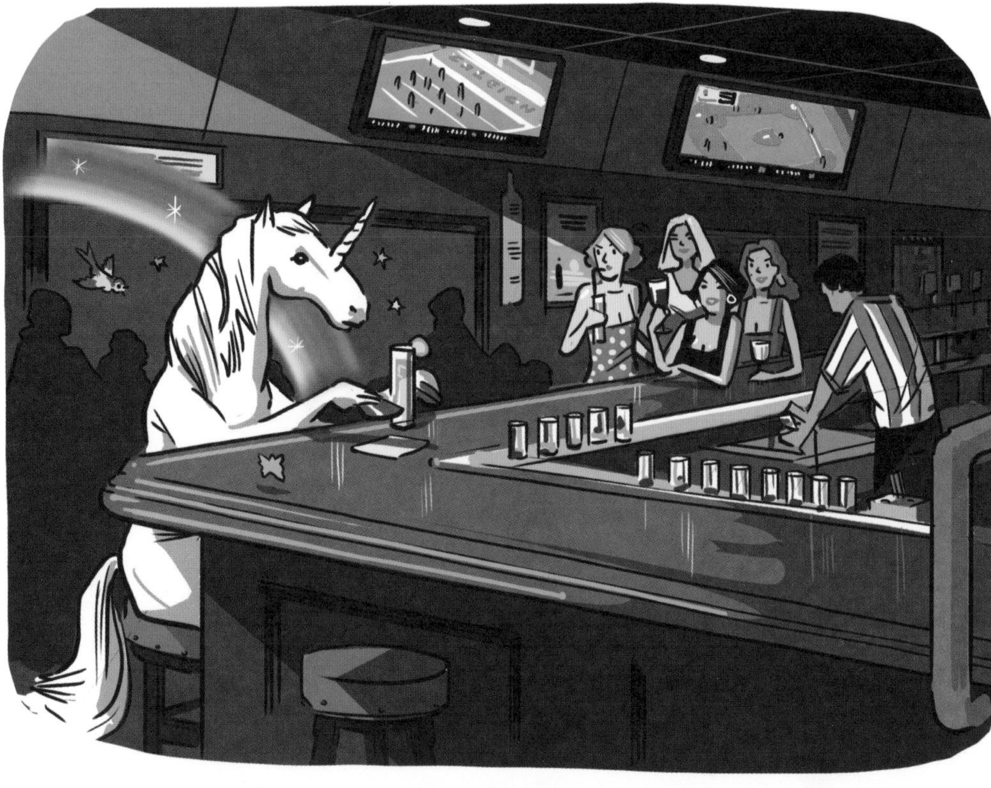

#18: Antenna

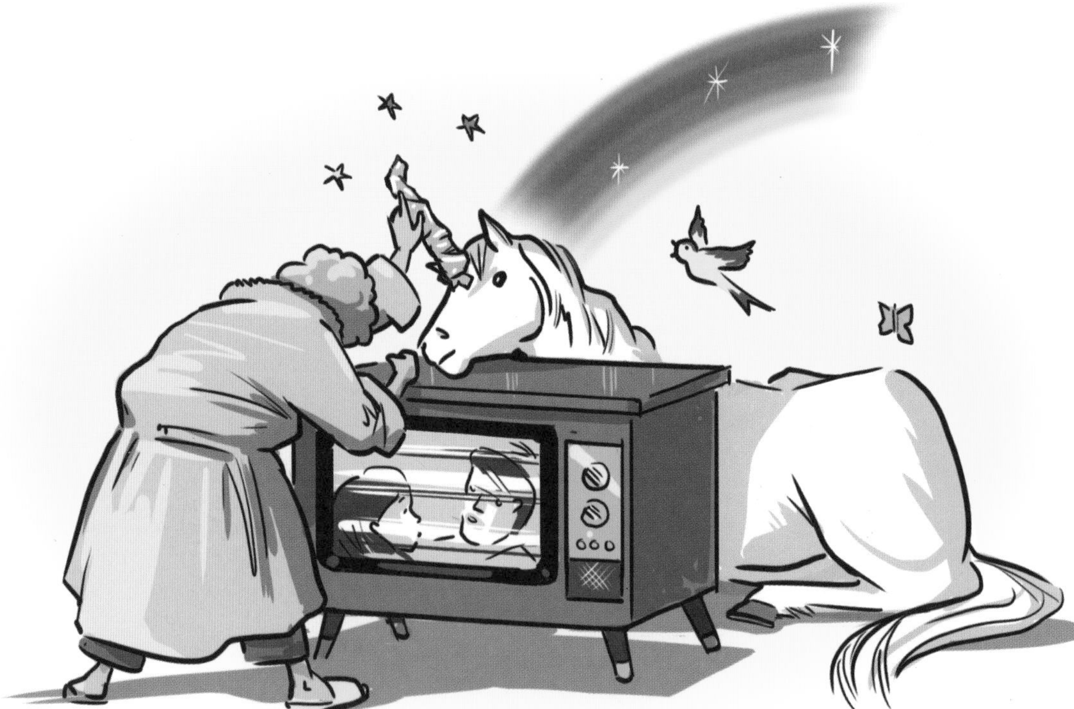

#19: Piñata

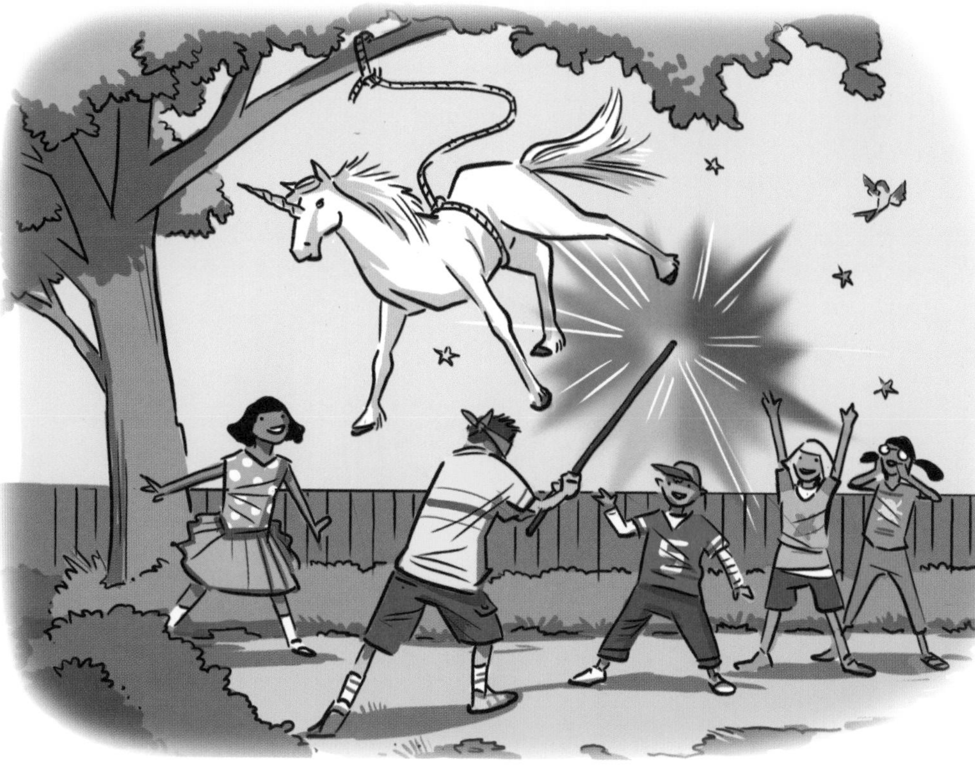

#20: Menorah

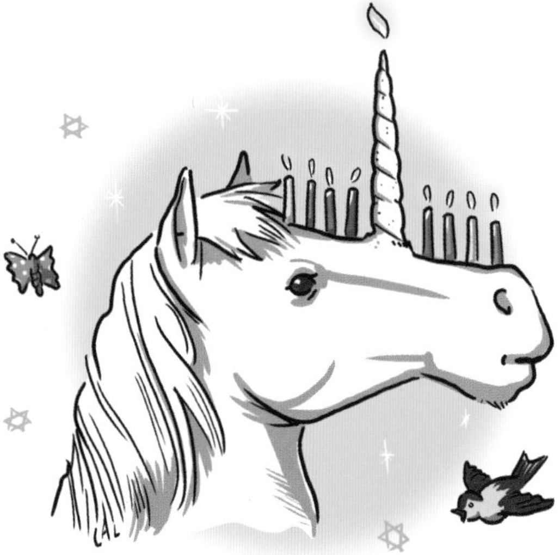

#21: Christmas Tree

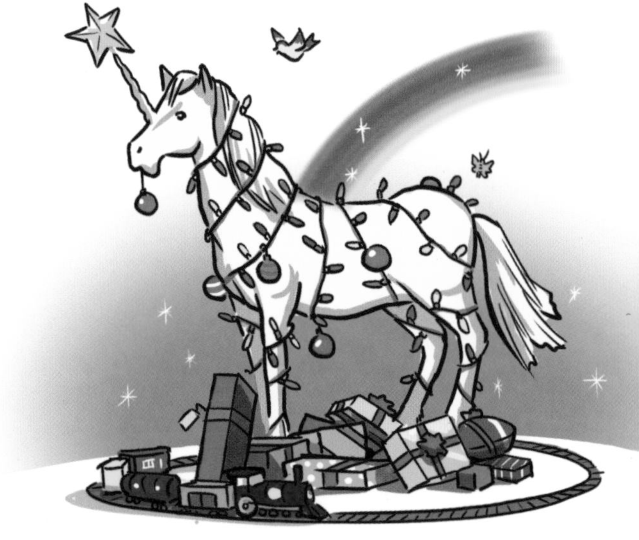

#22: Mall Rudolph

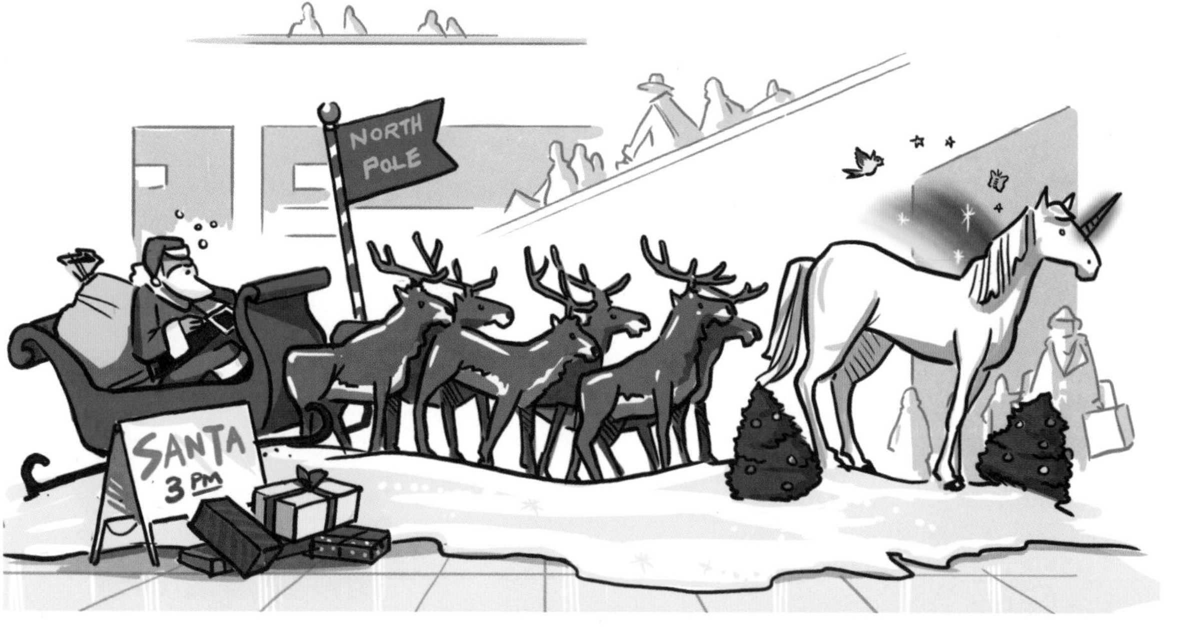

NORTH POLE
SANTA
3 PM

#23: Pool Boy

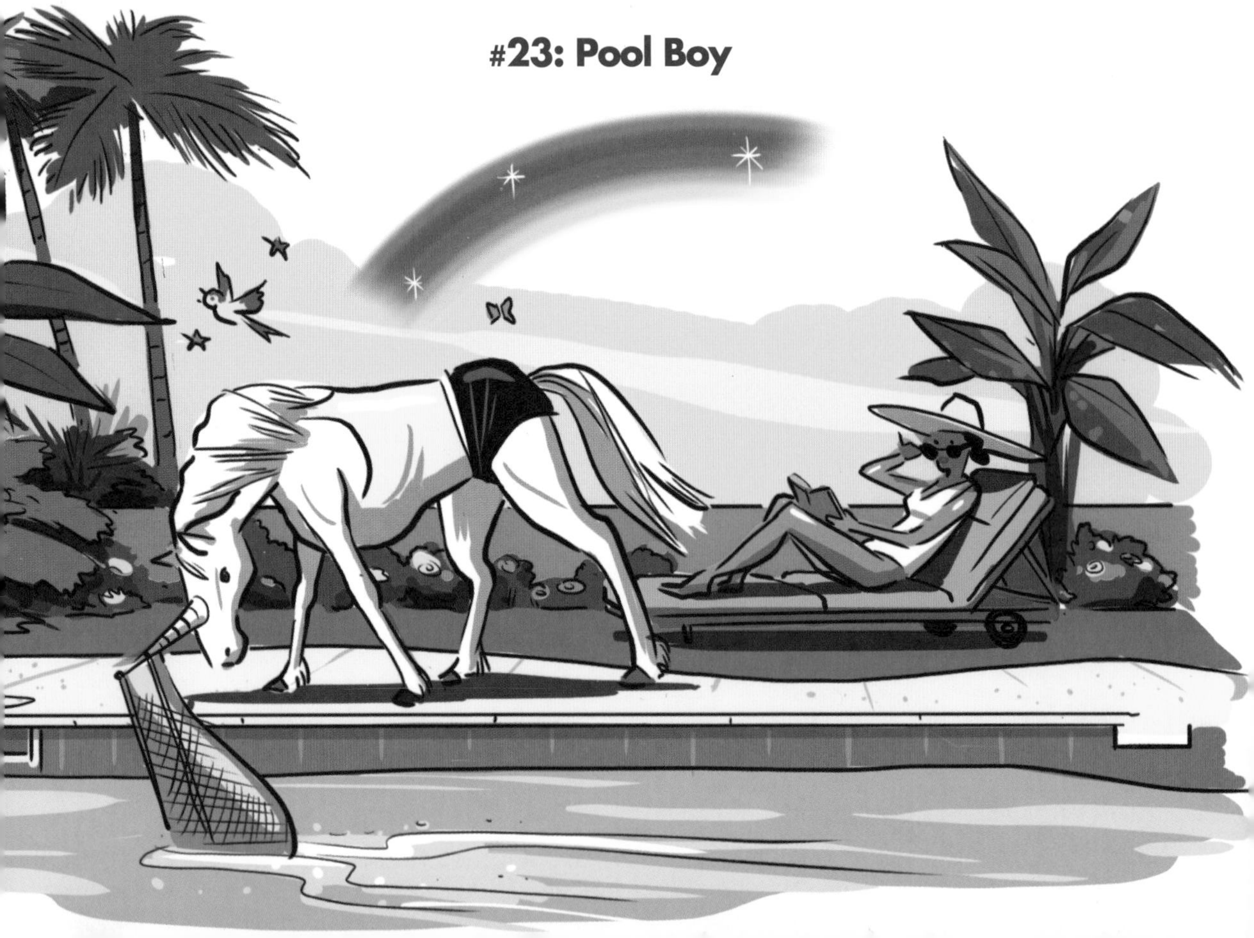

#24: Kabob

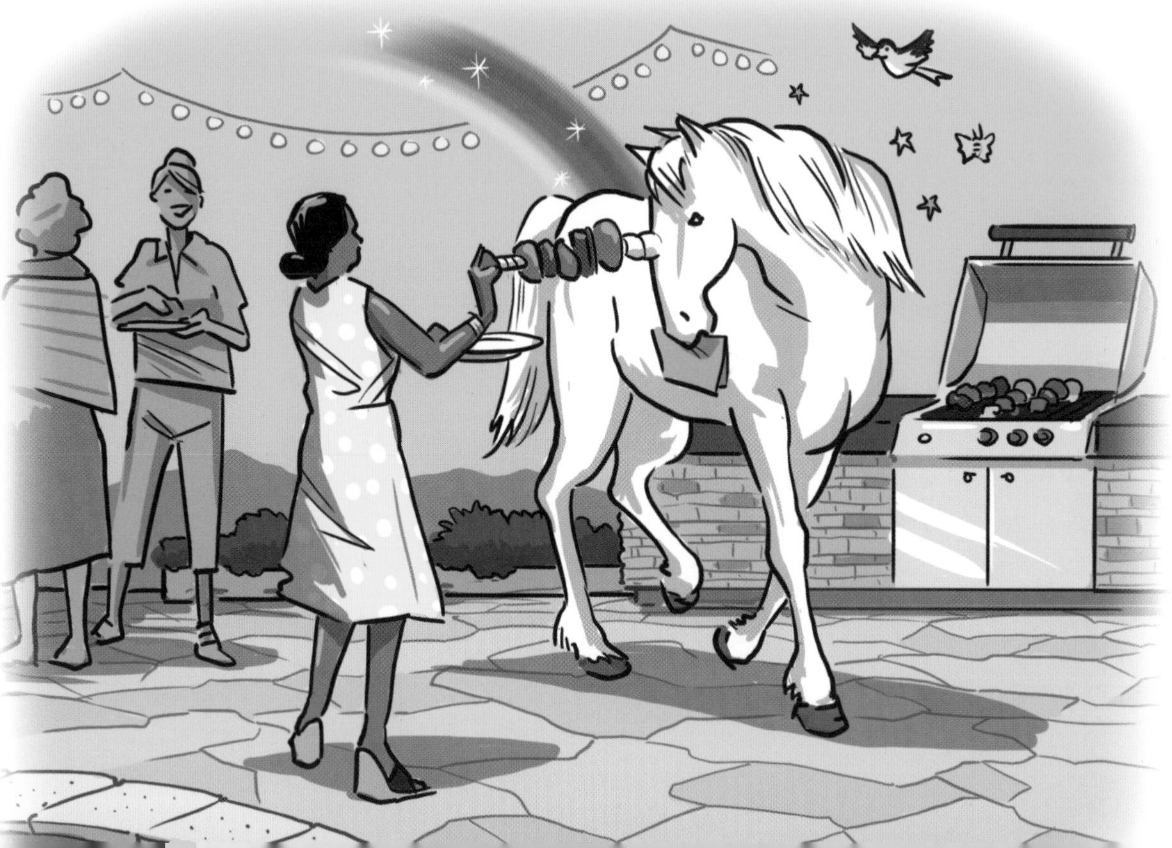

#25: Cable News Talking Head

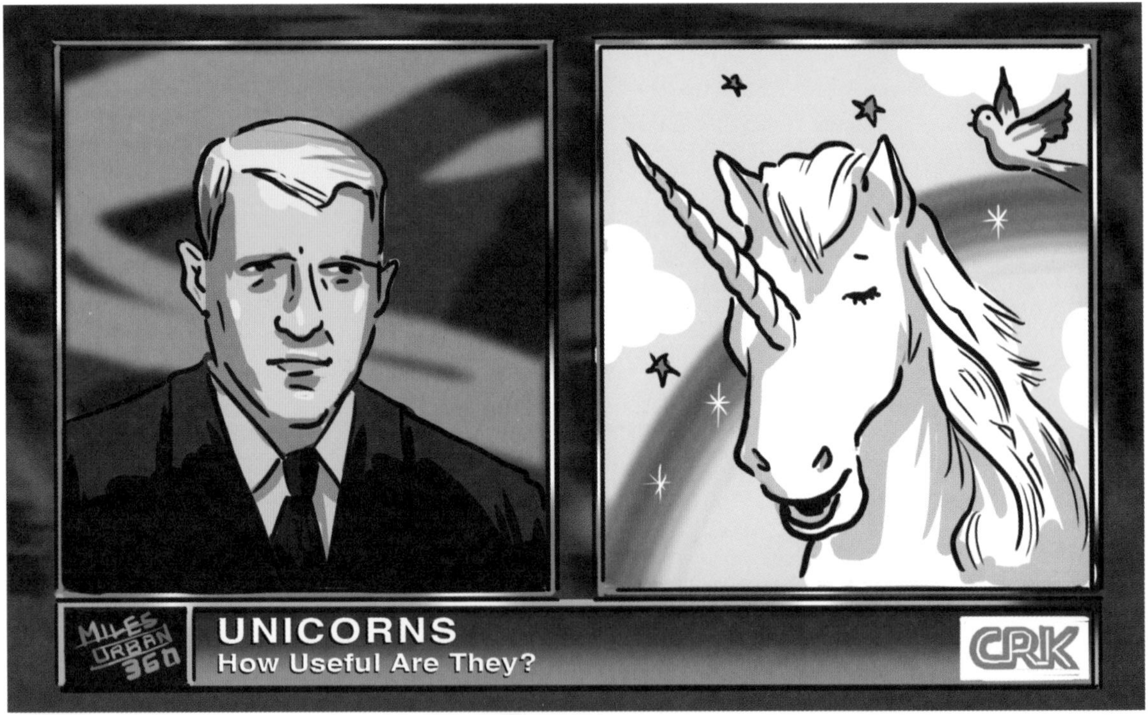
MILES URBAN 360
UNICORNS
How Useful Are They?
CRK

#26: Corporate Wonk

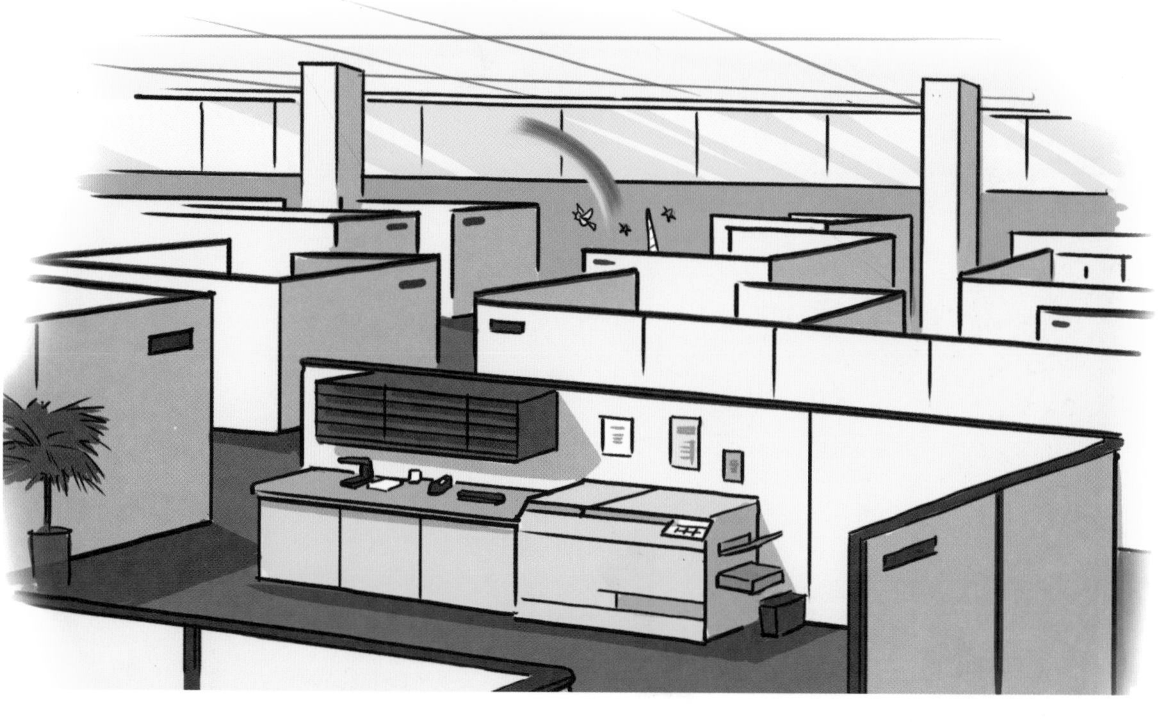

#27: Stake

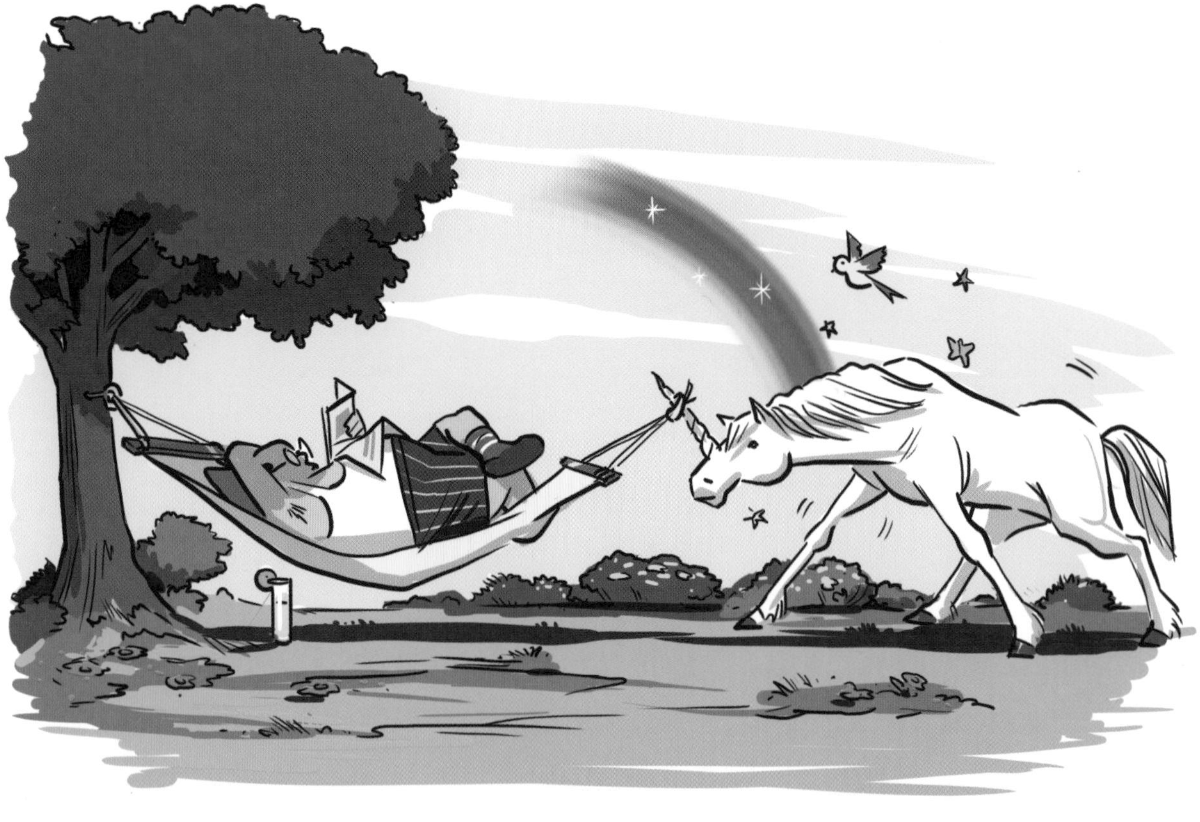

#28: Steak

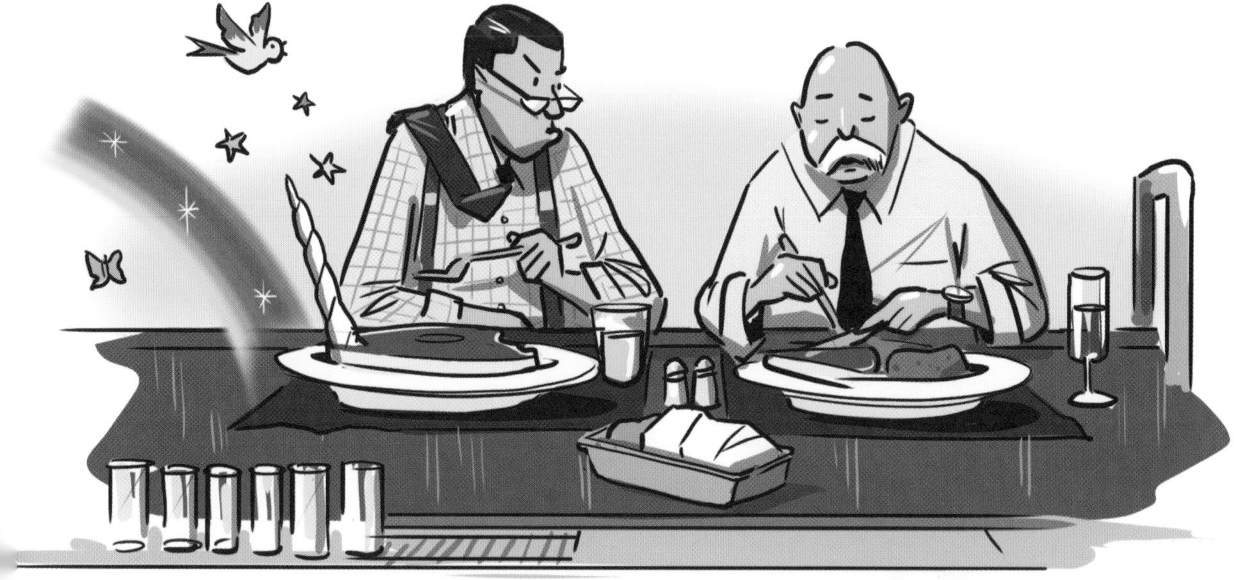

#29: Reboot

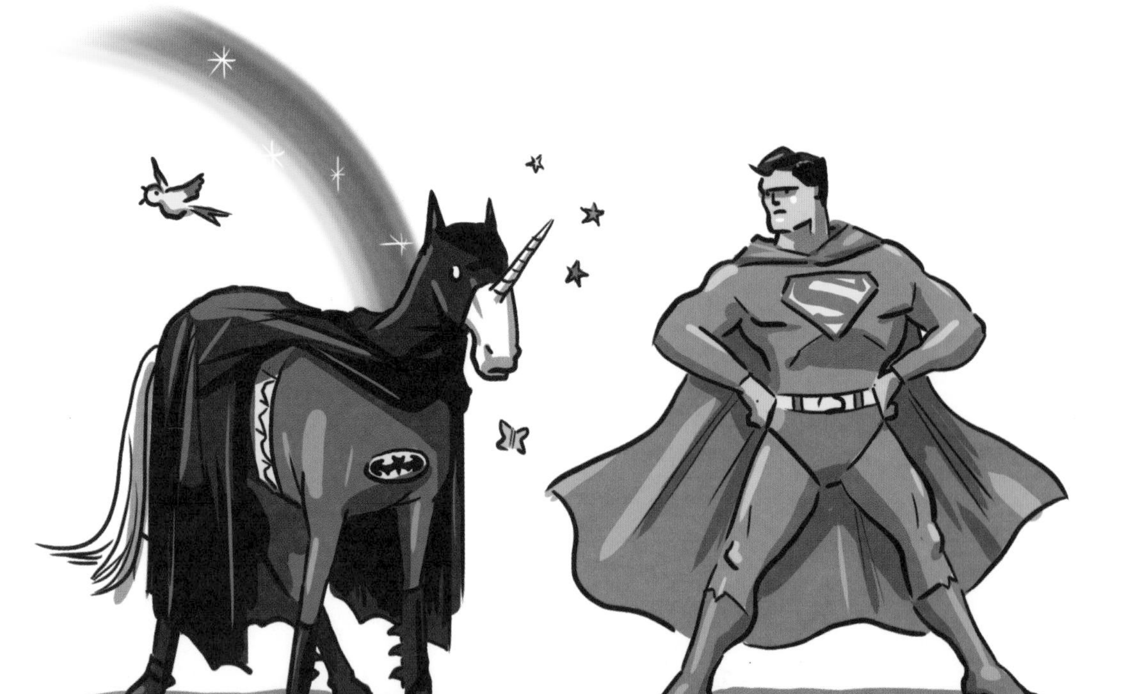

#30: Kaiju Killer

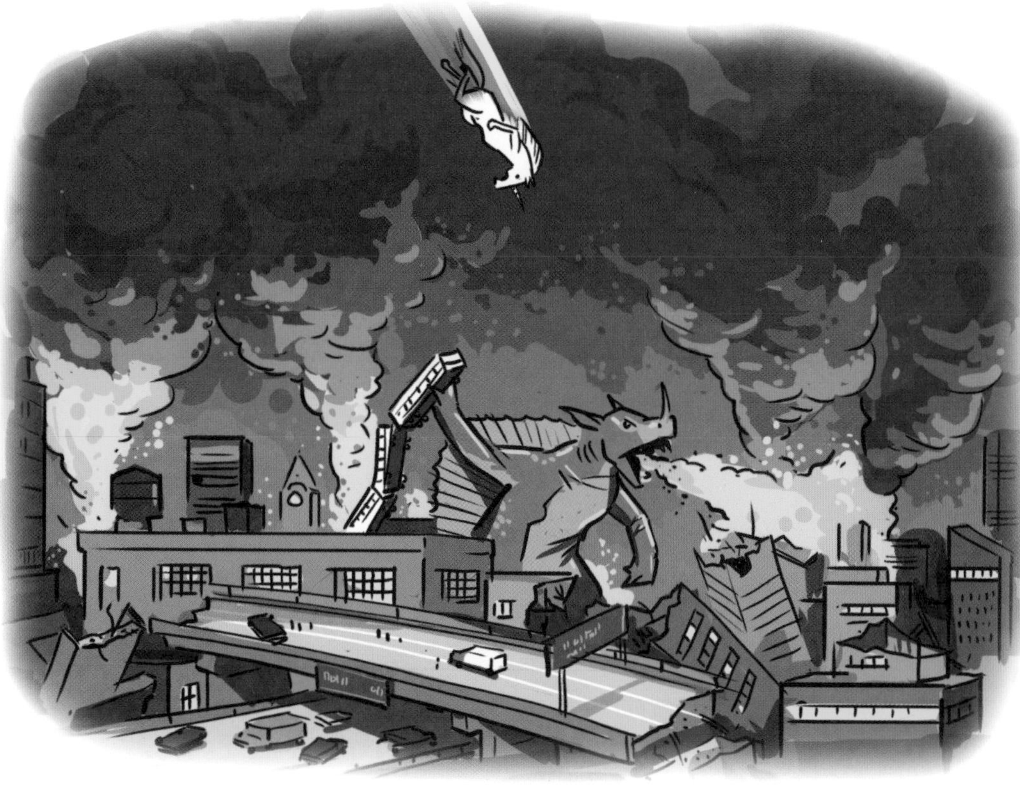

#31: Redshirt

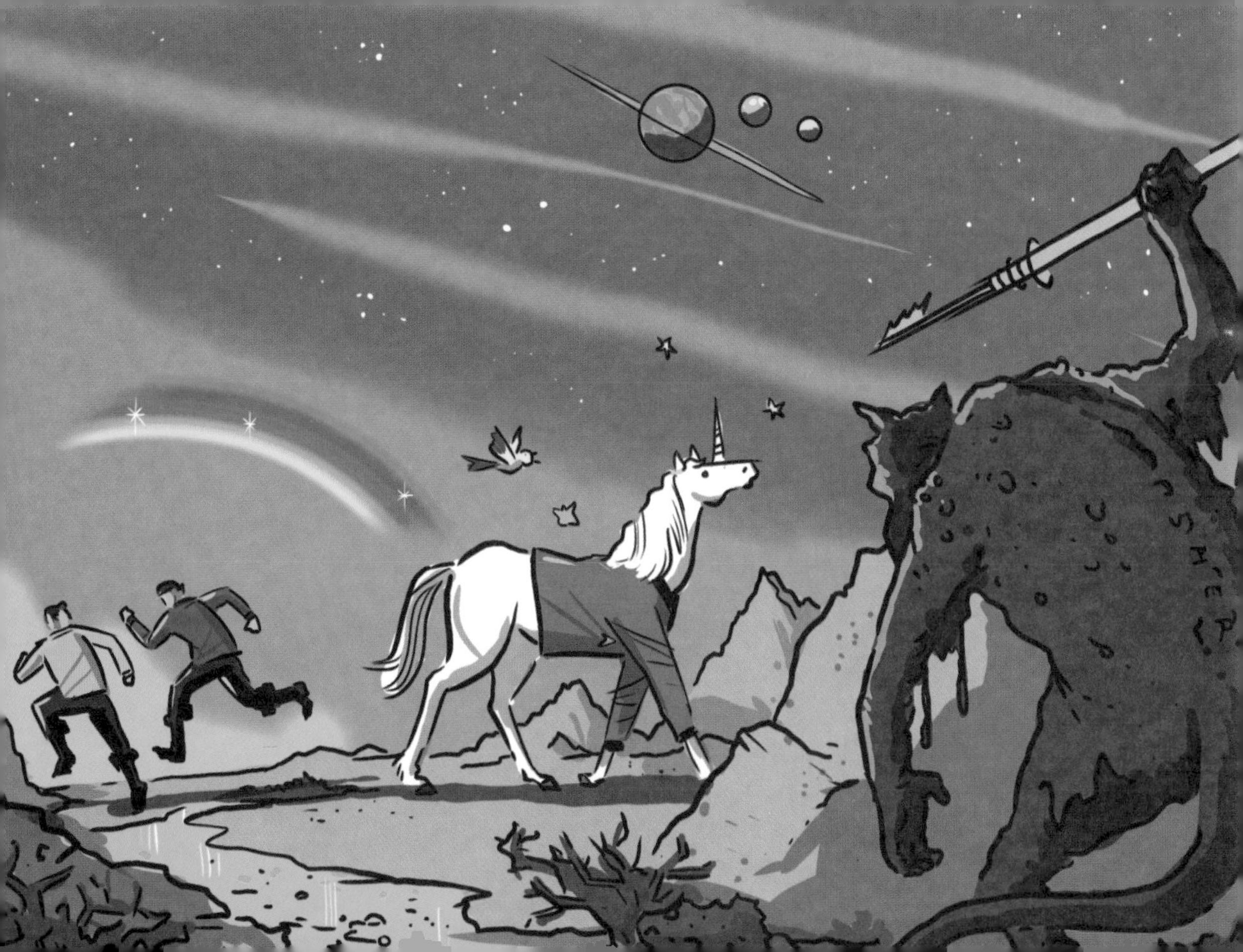

#32: Tire Gauge

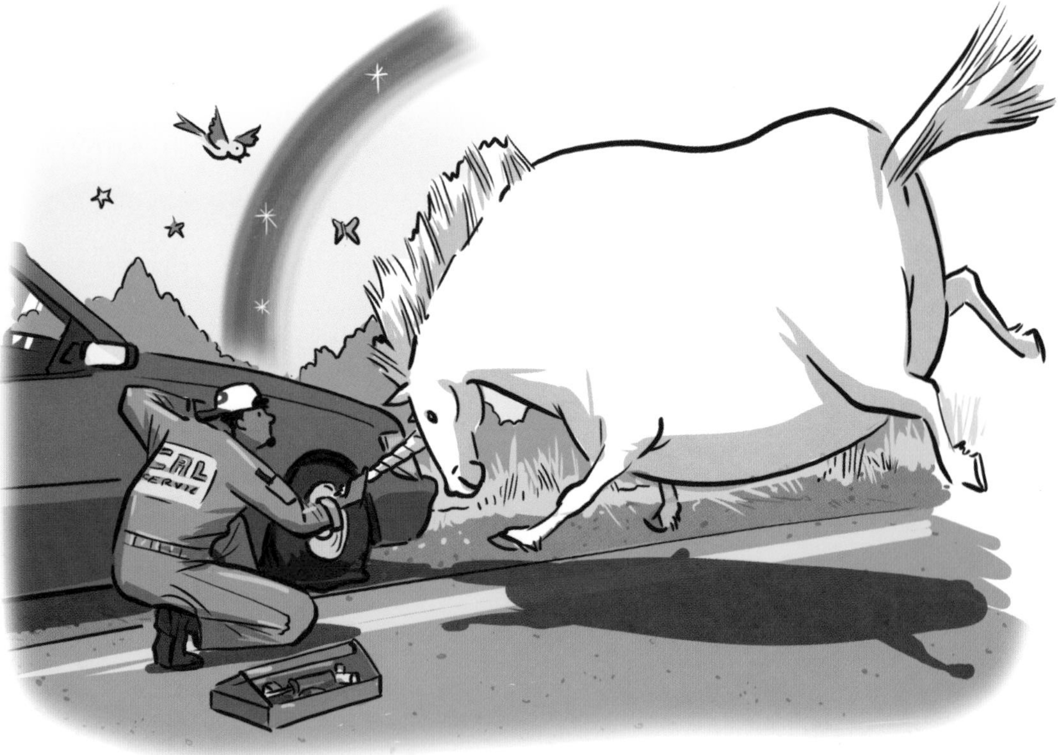

#33: Chauffeur

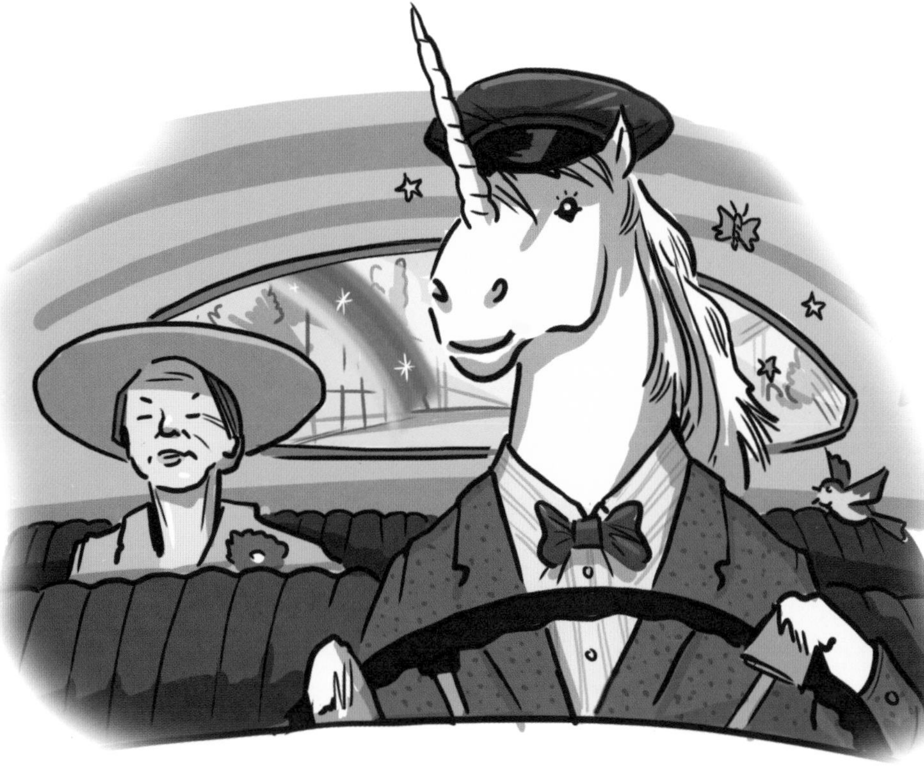

#34: Breathalyzer

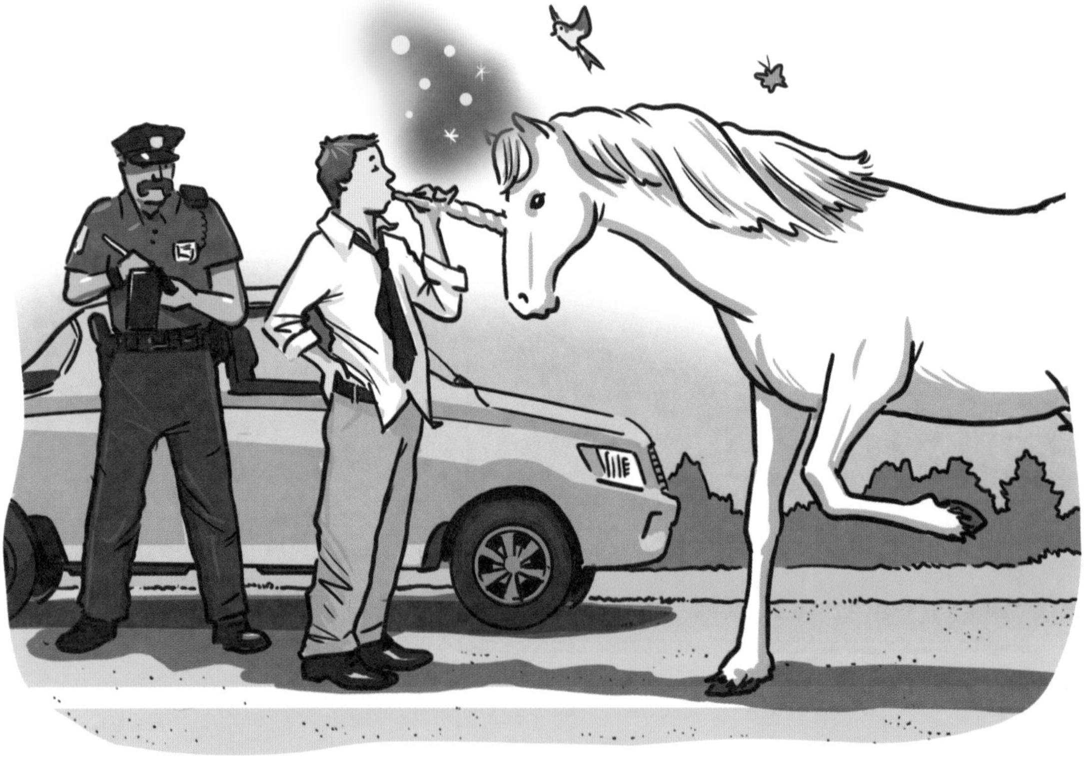

#35: Stick Shift

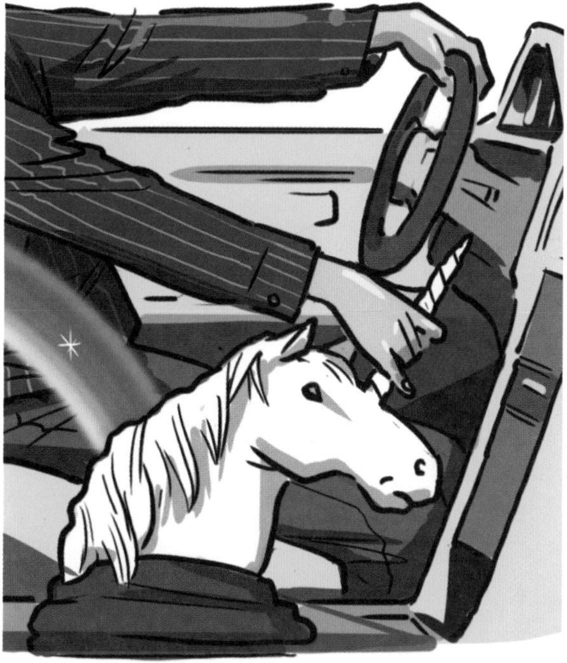

#36: Speedometer

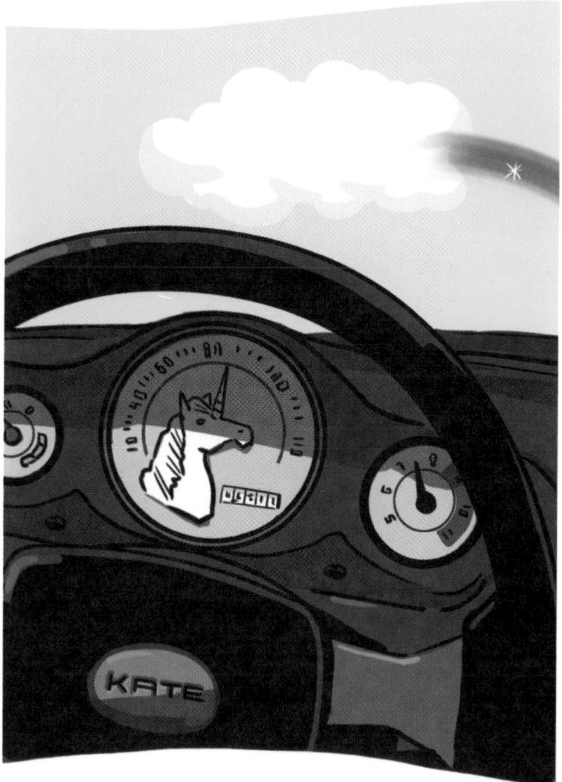
KATE

#37: Coat Rack

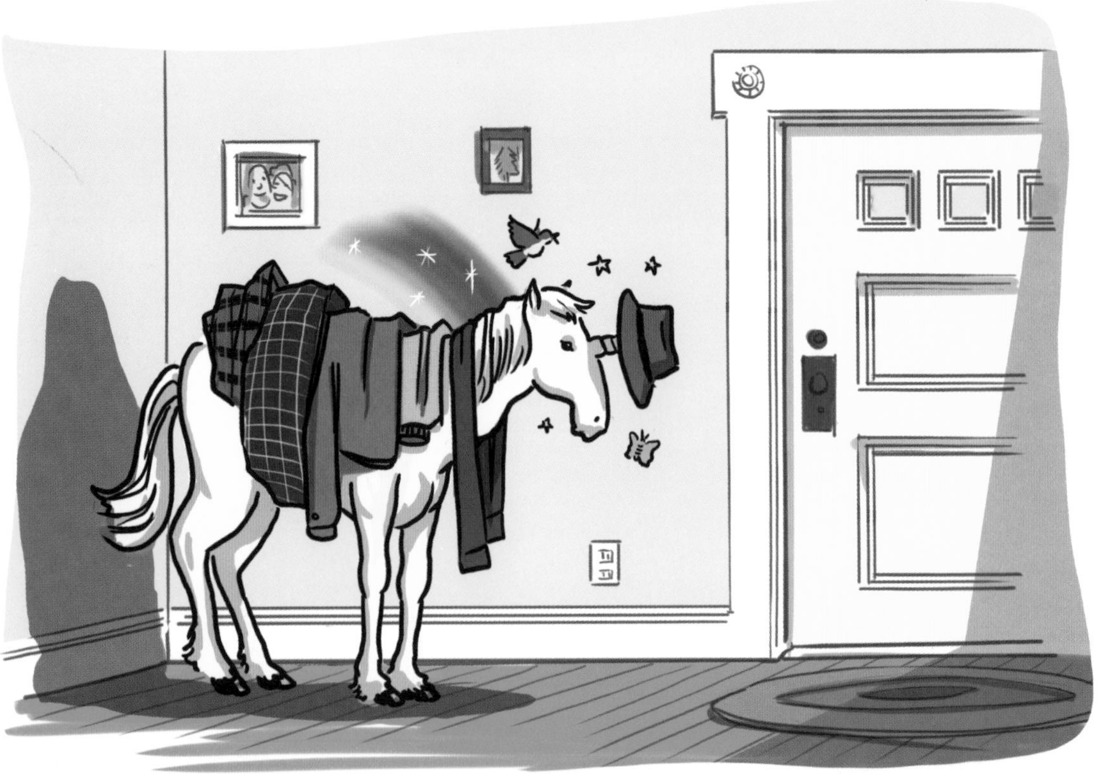

#38: Runner Up

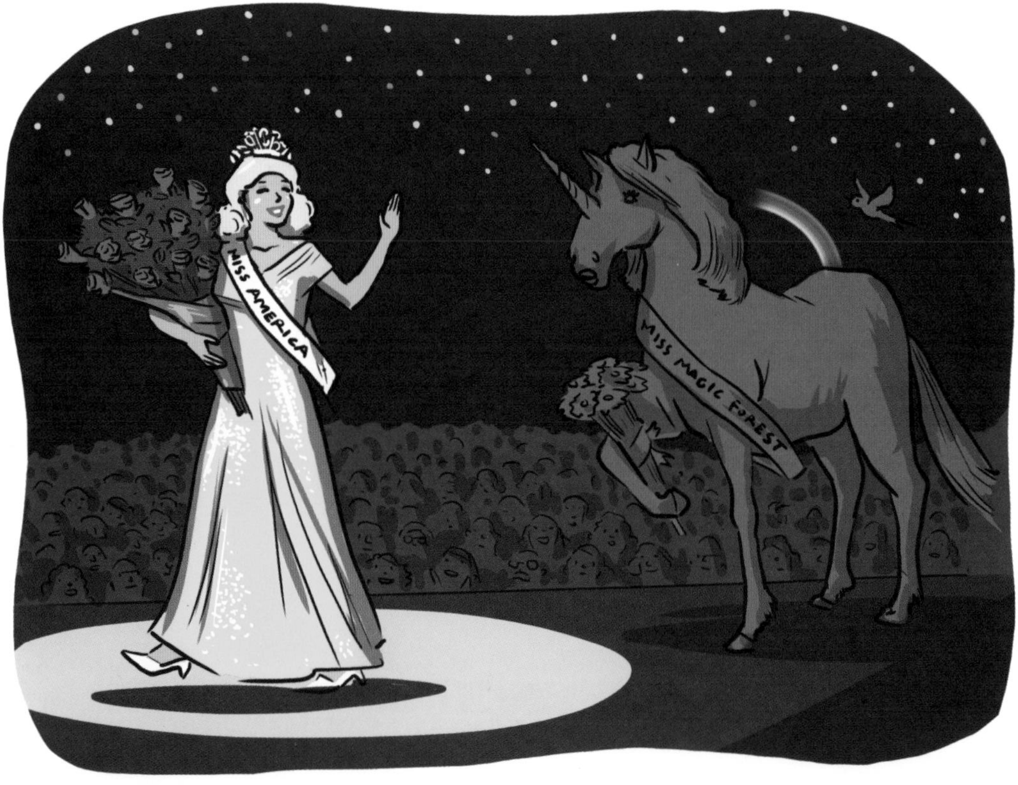

MISS AMERICA
MISS MAGIC FOREST

#39: Understudy

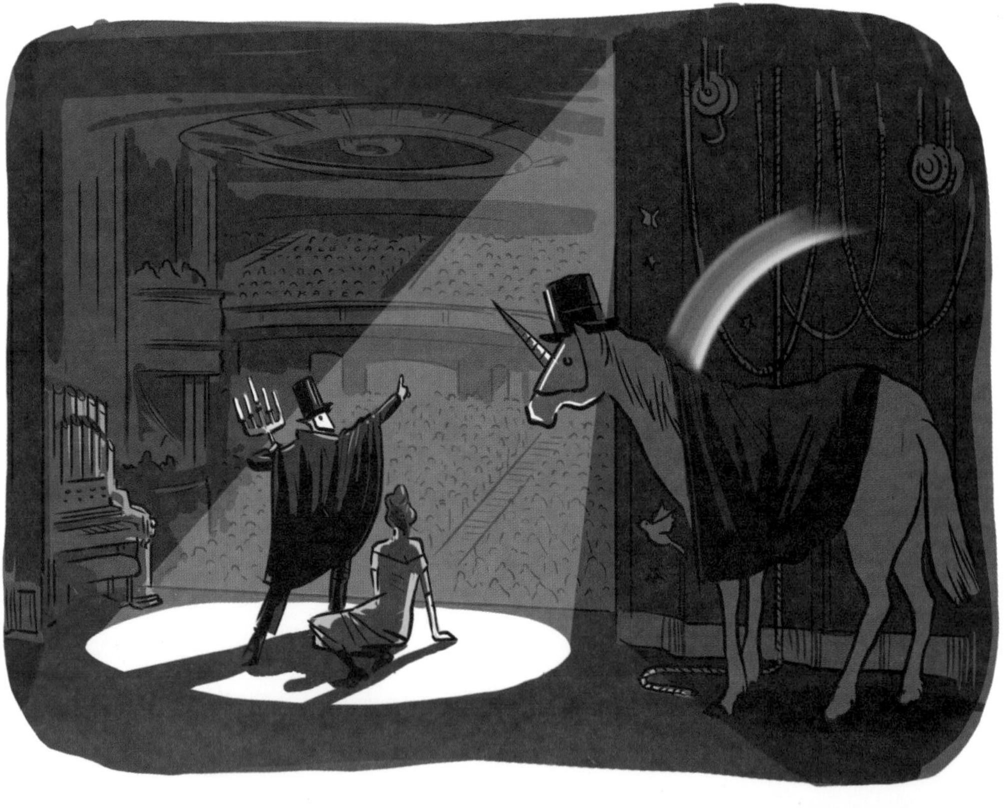

#40: Award Ceremony Seat-filler

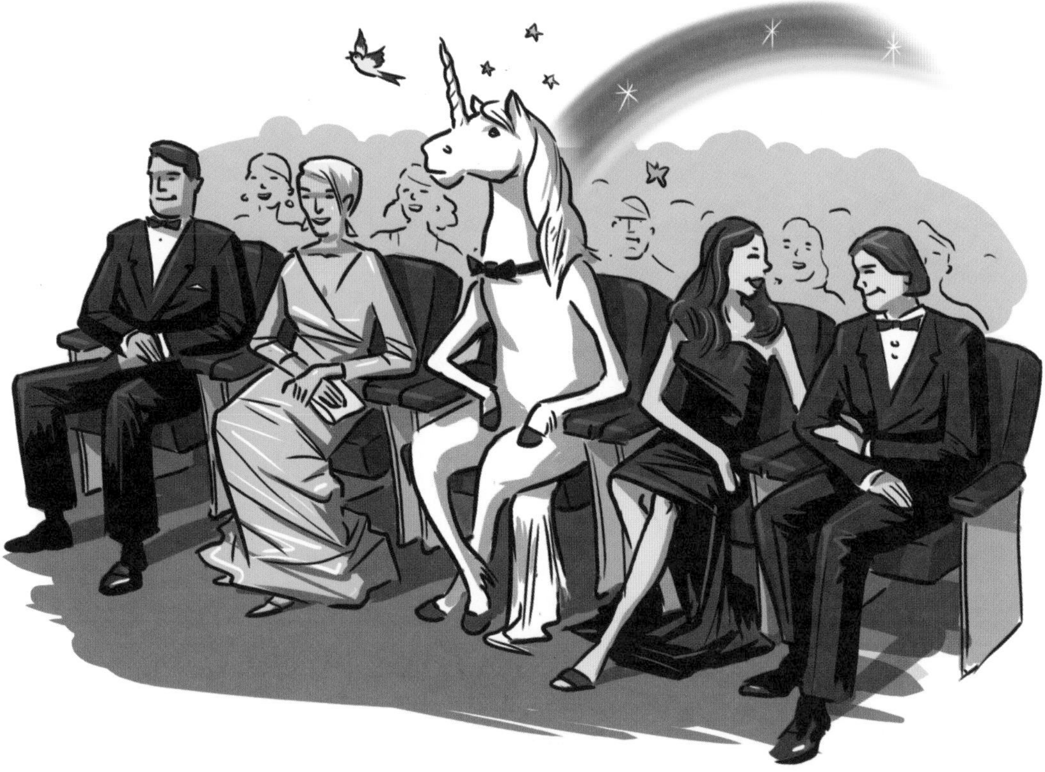

#41: Plumber

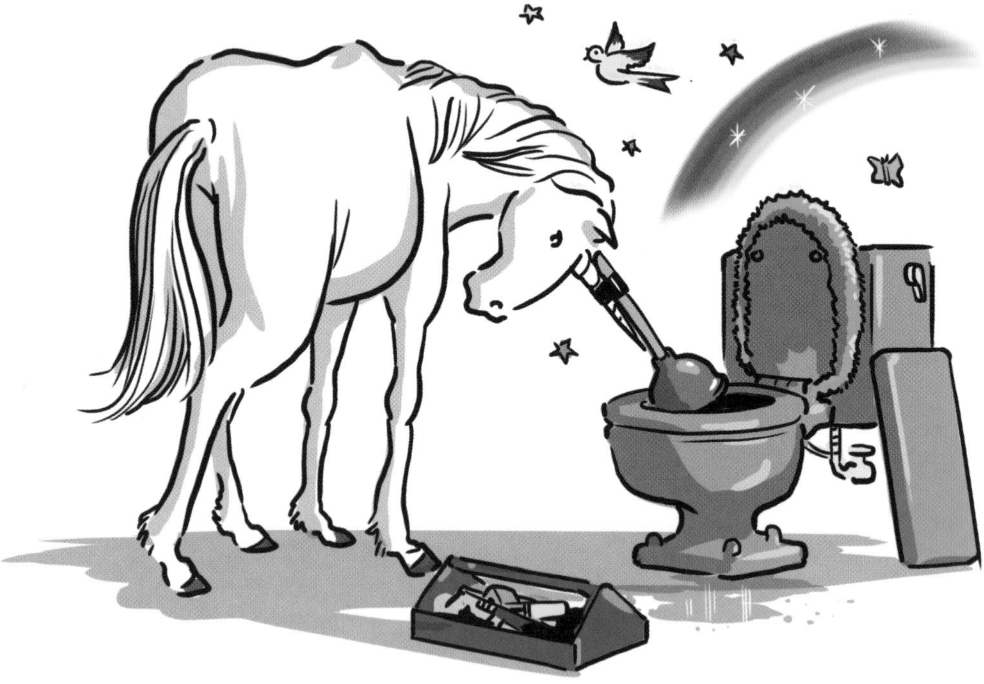

#42: Cake Slicer

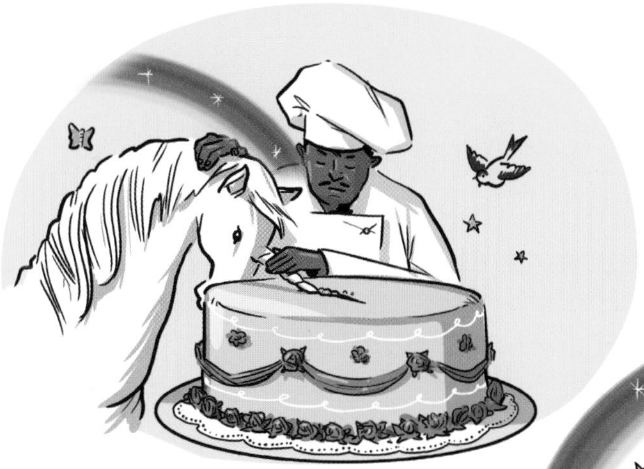

#43: Back Scratcher

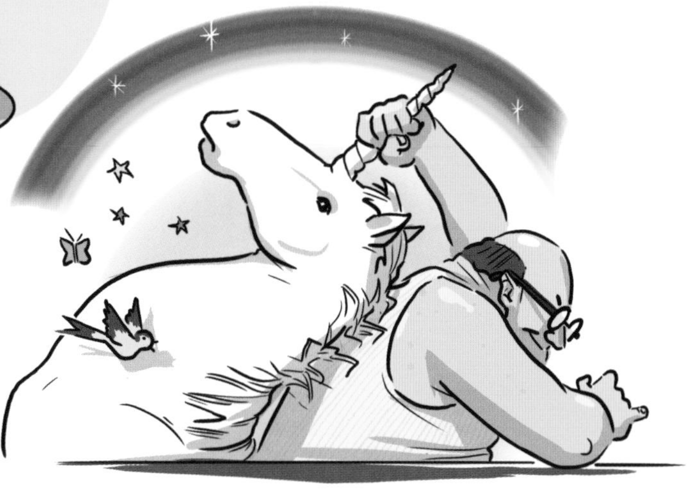

#44: Stirrer

#45: Ice Pick

#46: Ice Breaker

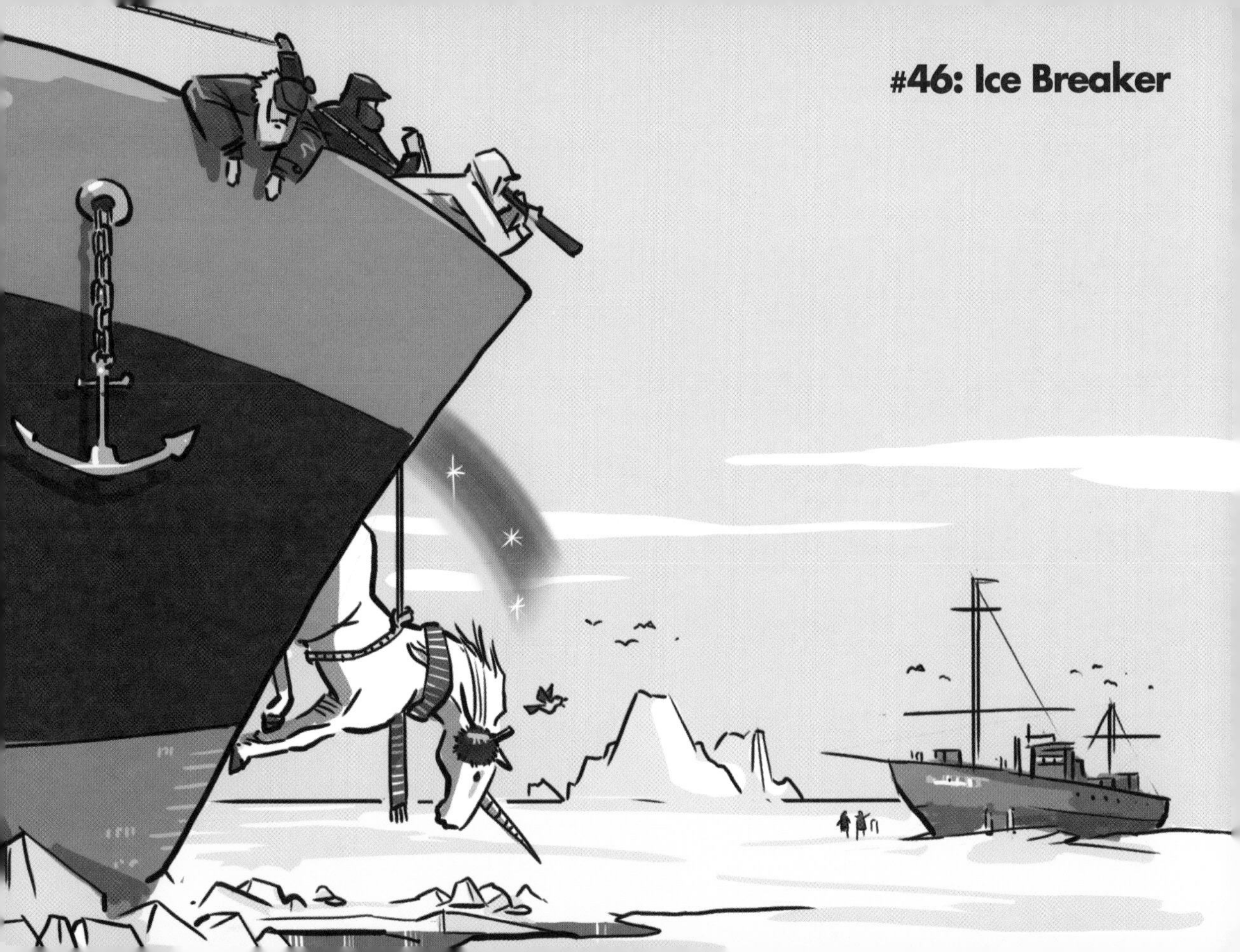

#47: Toilet Paper Holder

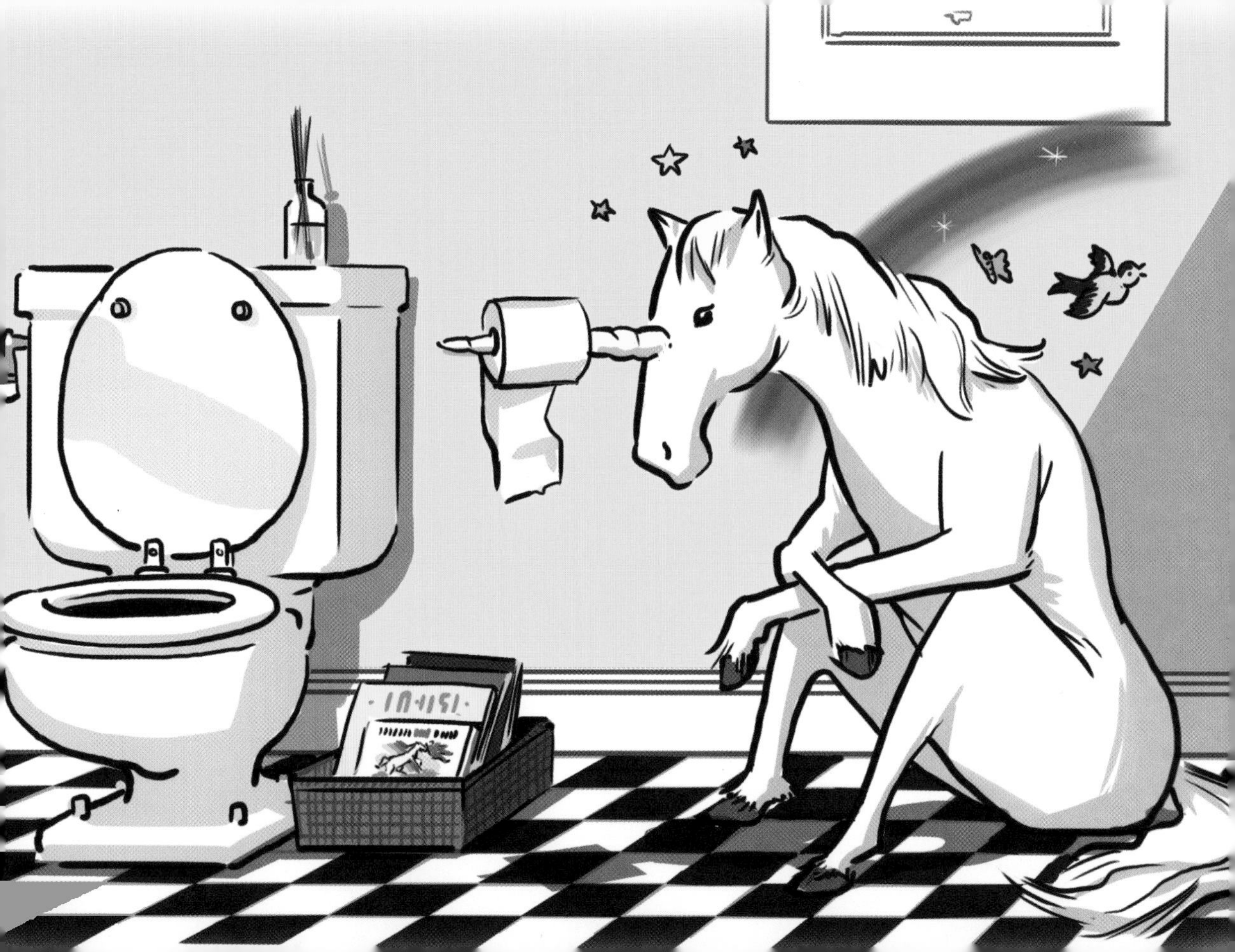

#48: Goalie

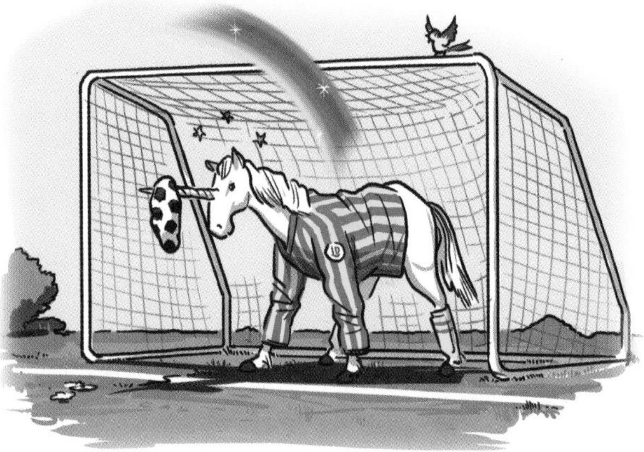

#49: Tee

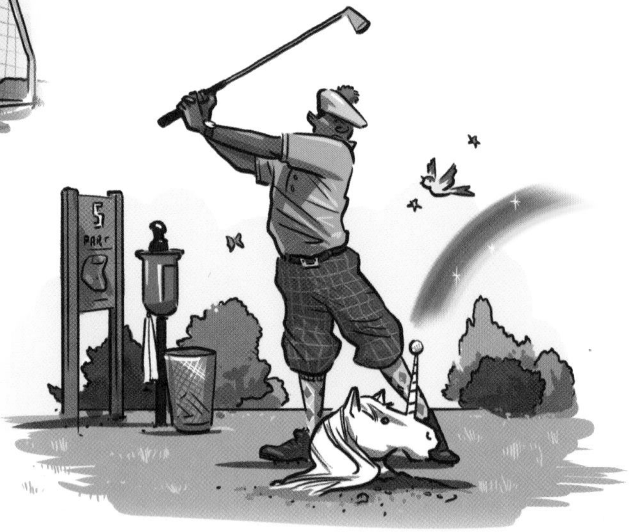
5
PAR

#50: Pinch Hitter

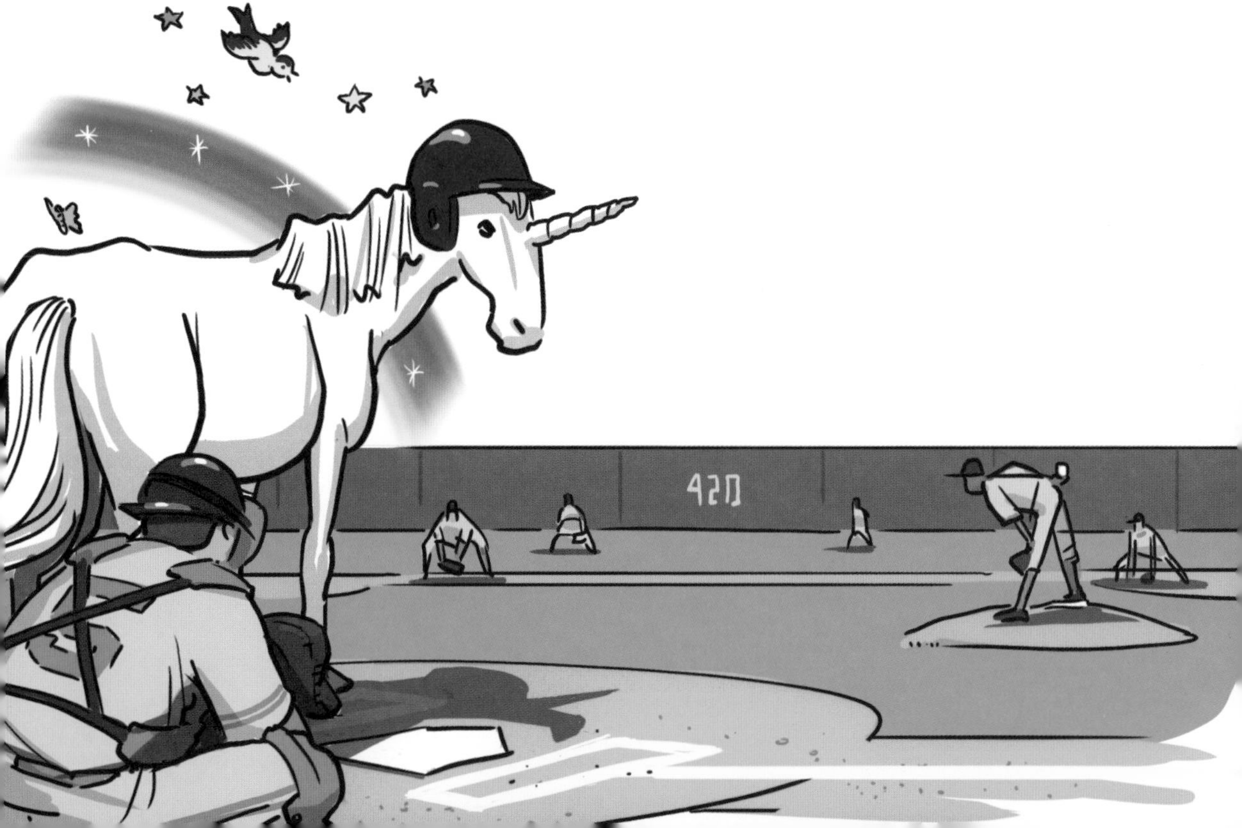

420

#51: Scapegoat

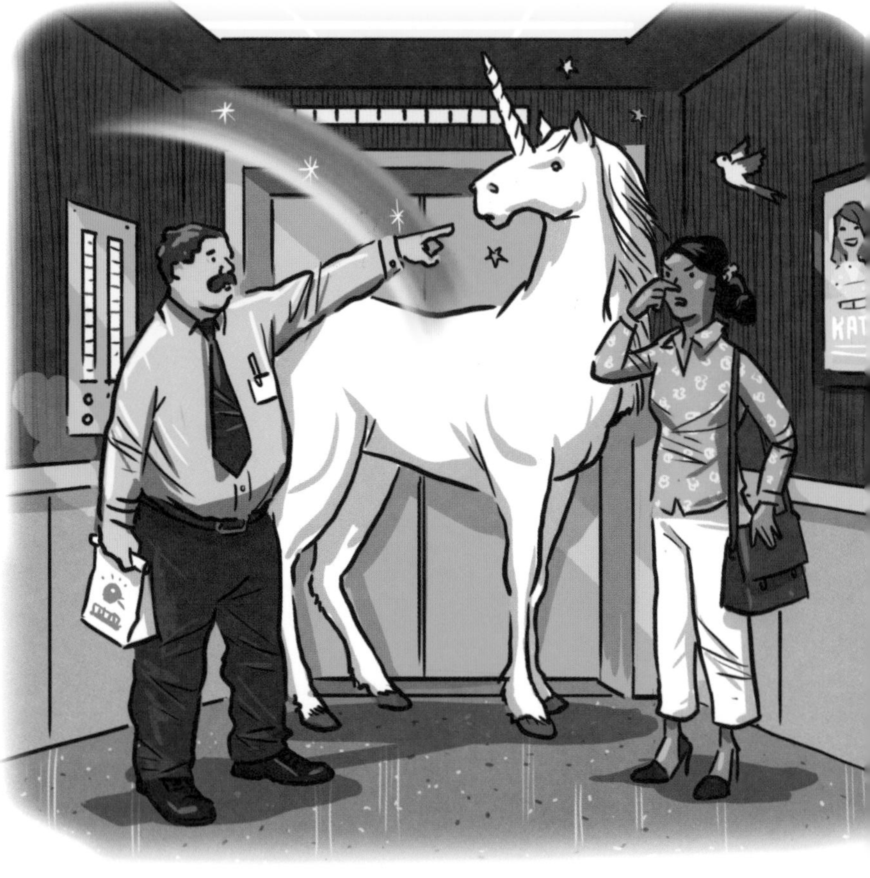

#52: Shoehorn

#53: Deal Breaker

#54: Photobomber

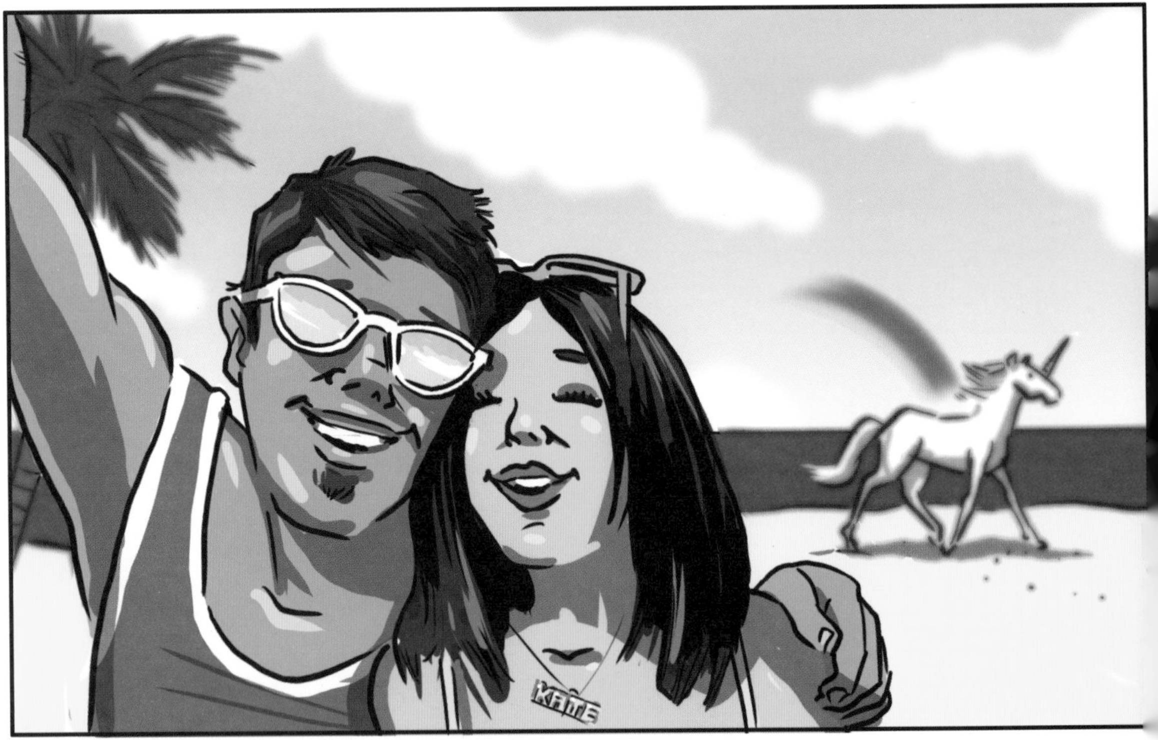
KATE

#55: Online Dating Avatar

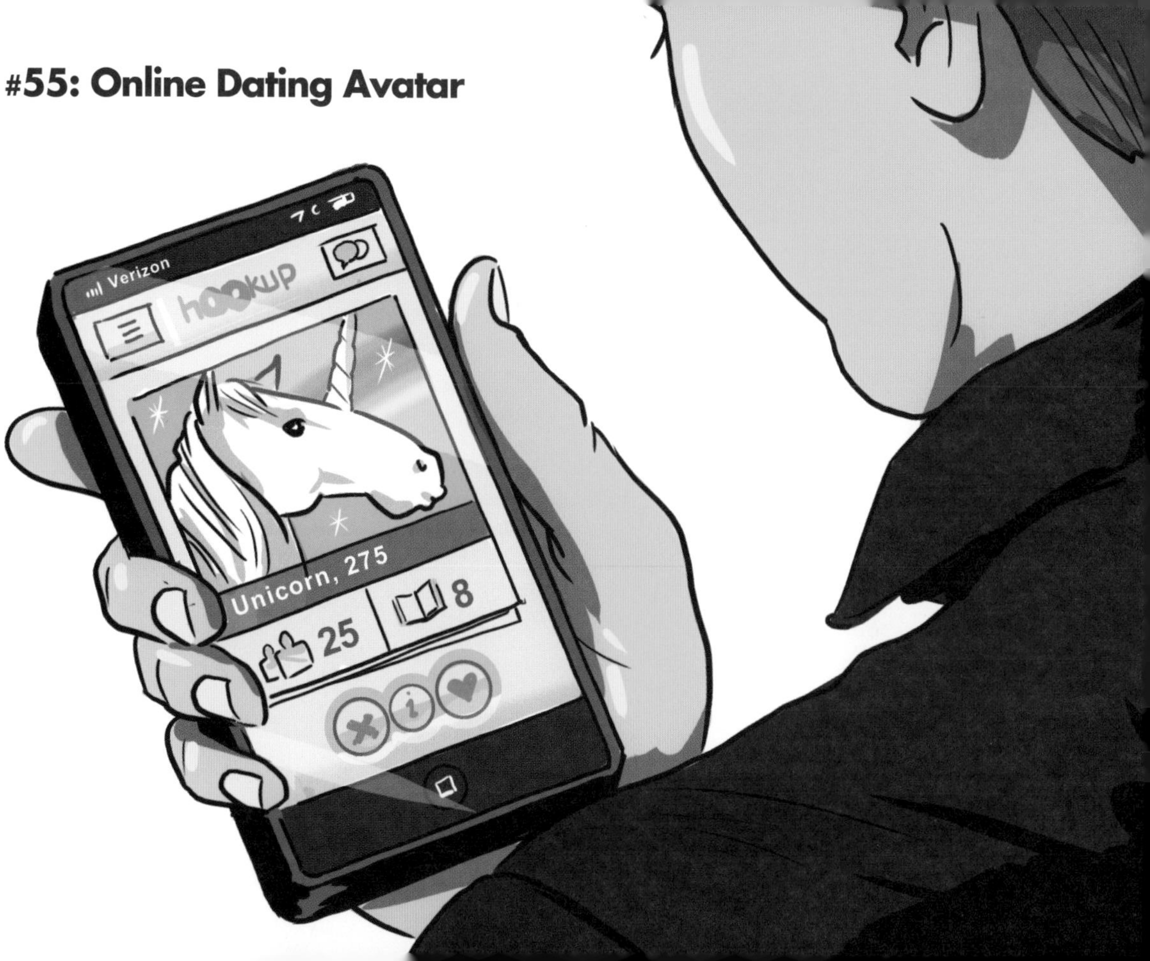
Verizon
hookup
Unicorn, 275
8
25

#56: Maypole

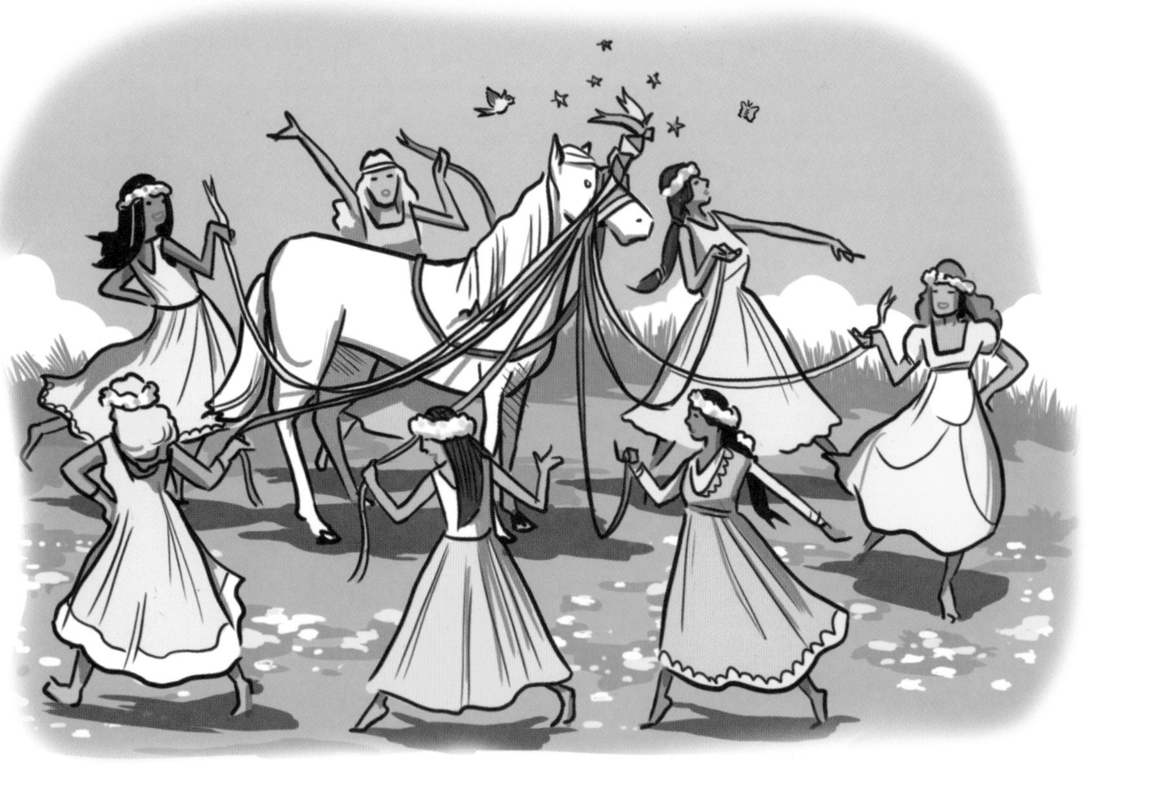

#57: Rainbow Maker

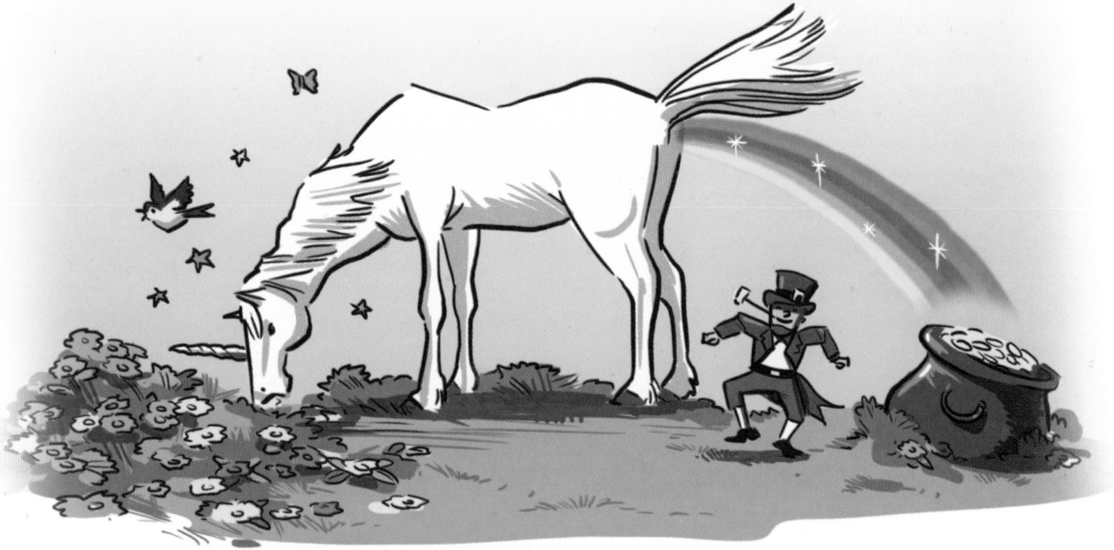

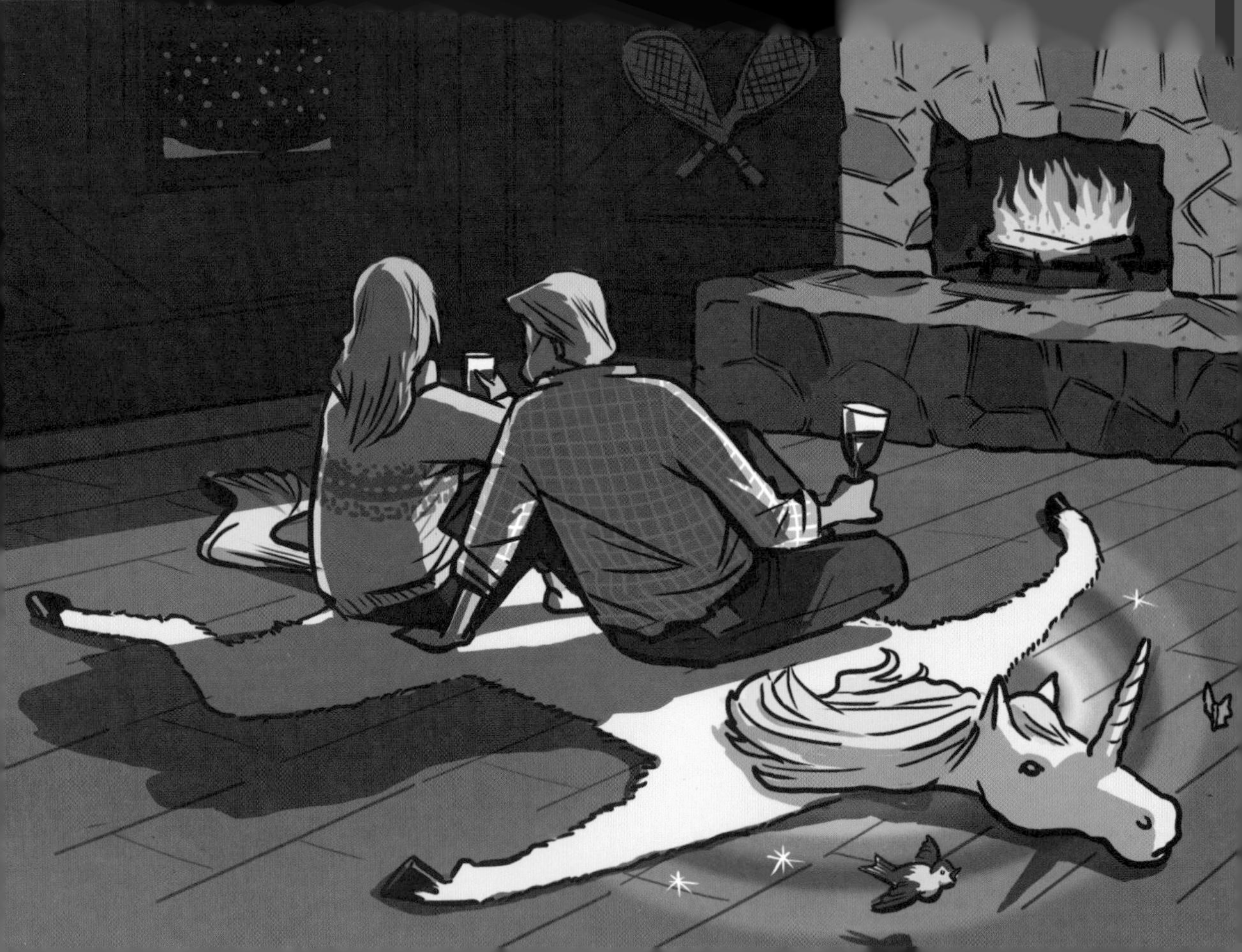

#58: Area Rug

#59: Room Décor

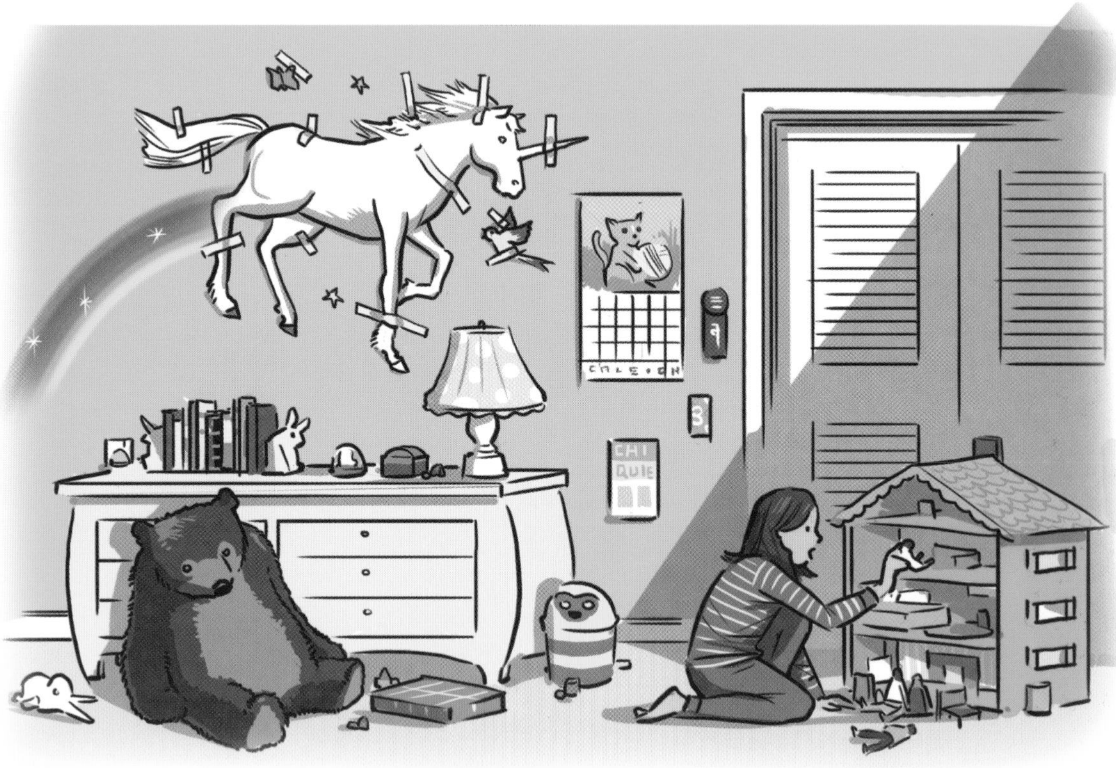

#60: Shawshanking

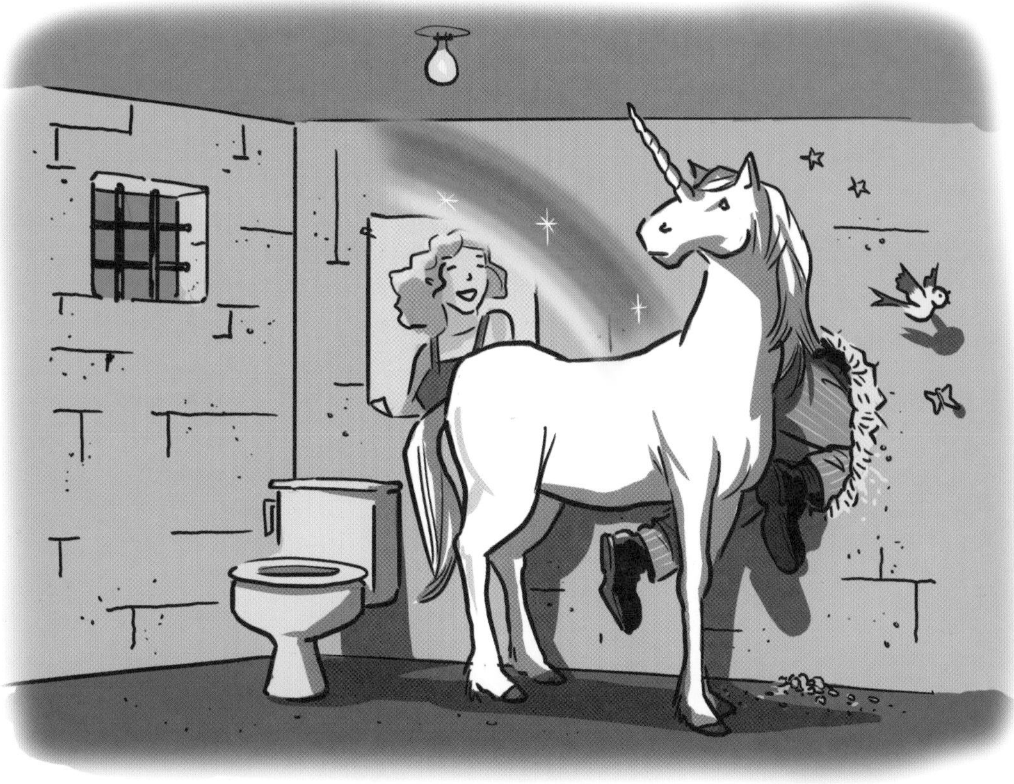

#61: Horny

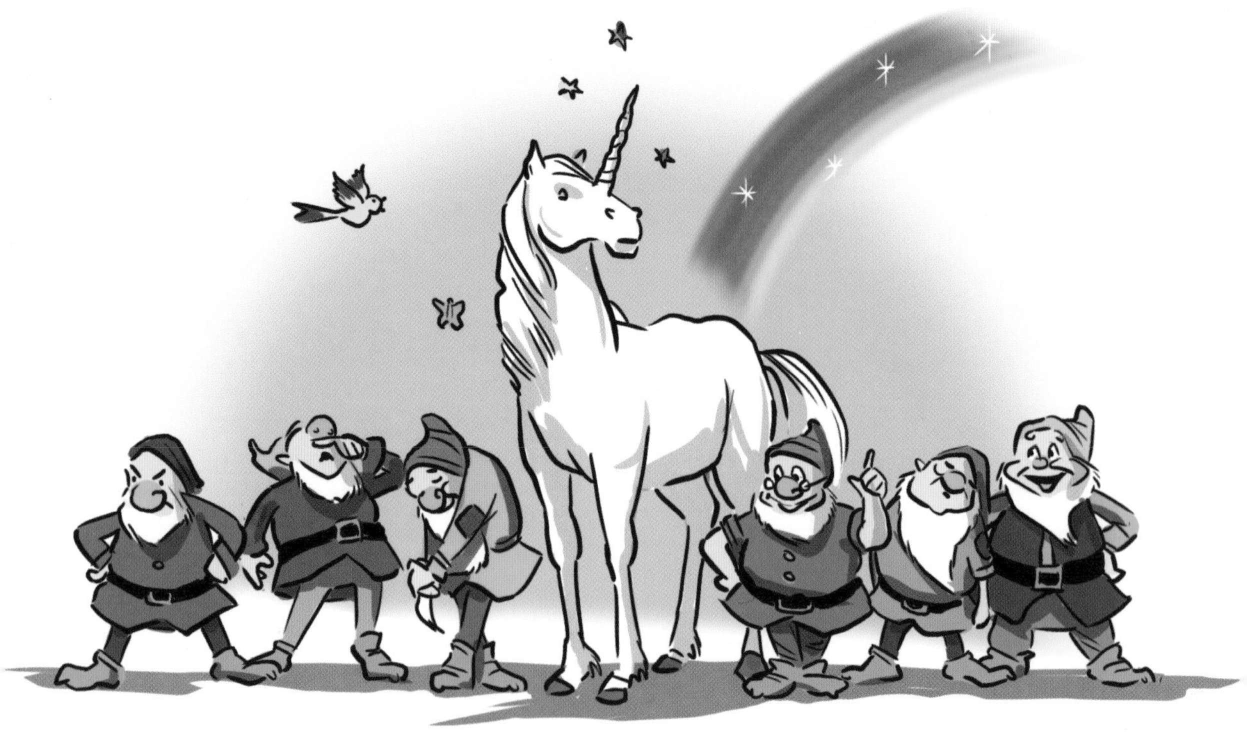

#62: Jedi

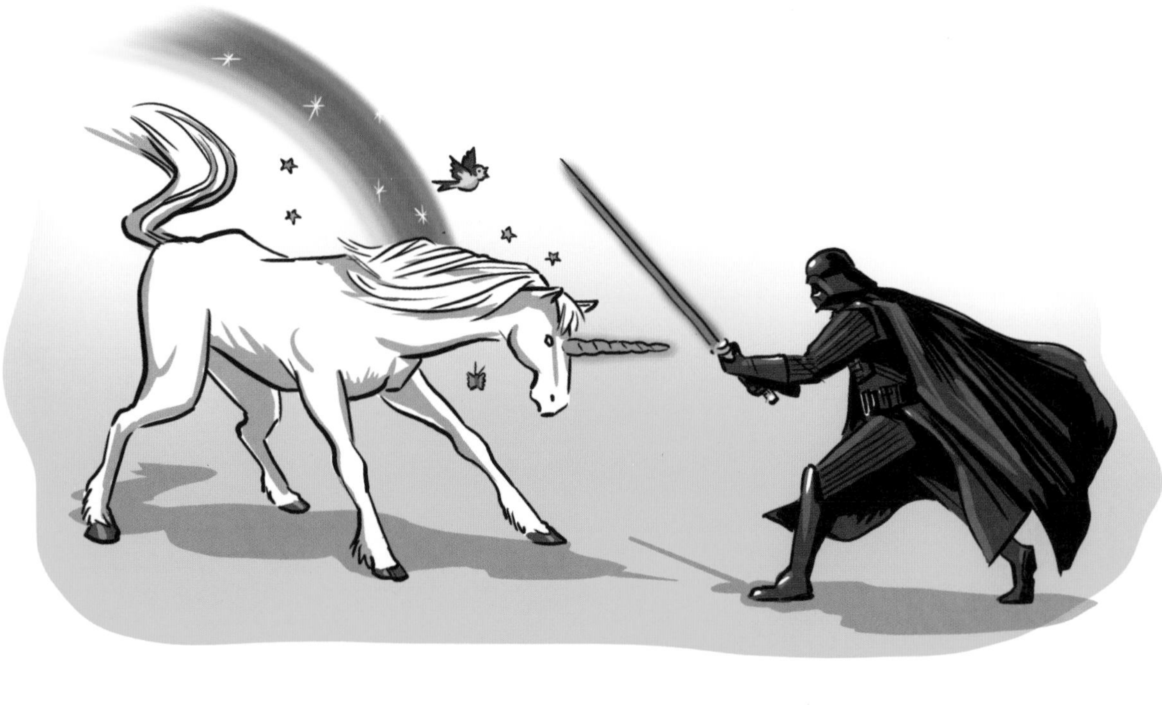

#63: Hunger Games

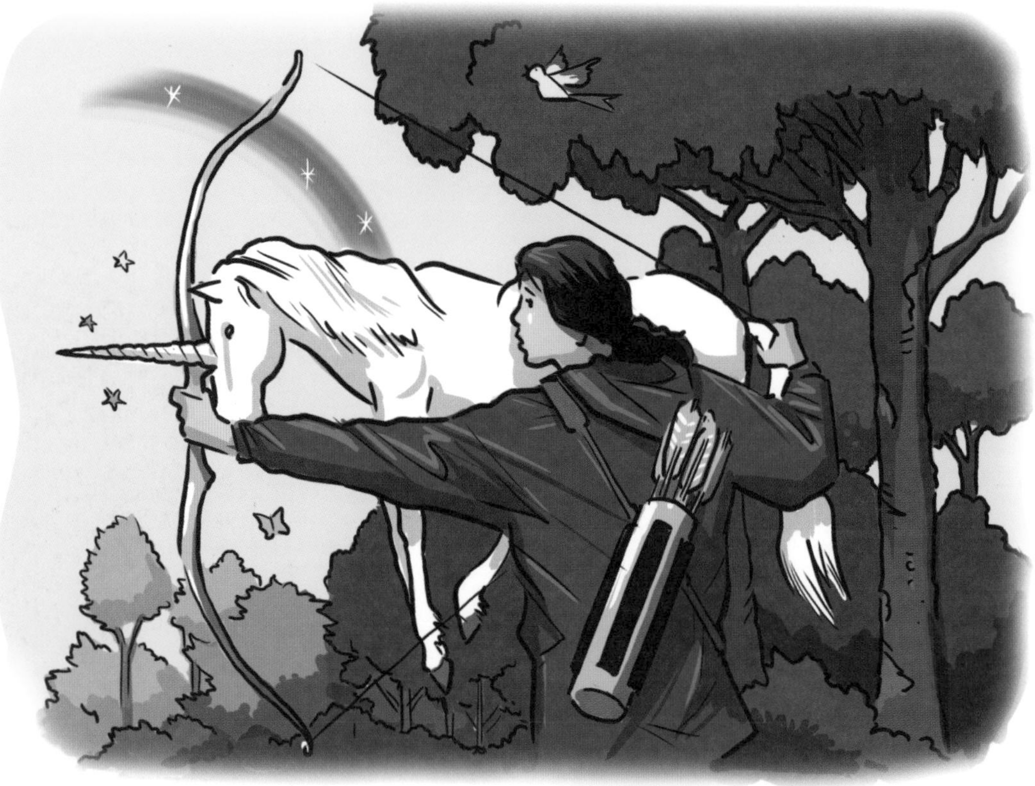

#64: Portrait Model

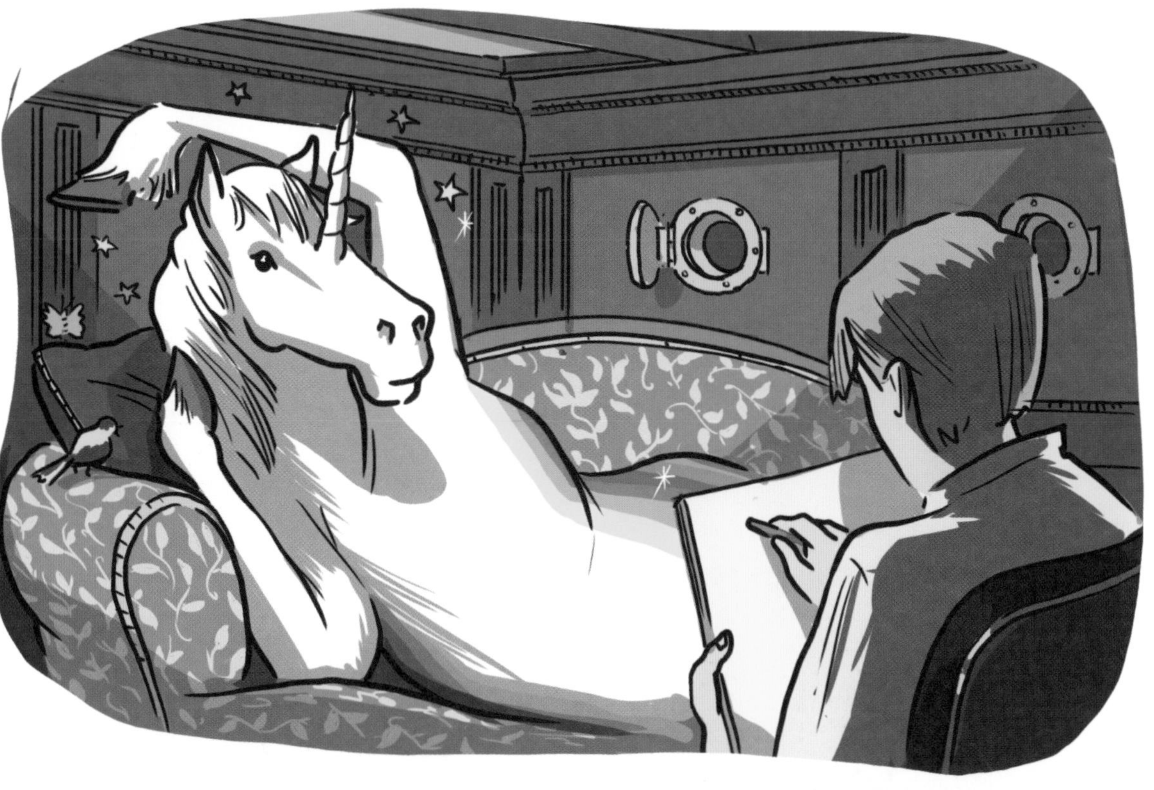

#65: Political Party Symbol

#66: Status Symbol

#67: Plastic Surgery "After" Photo

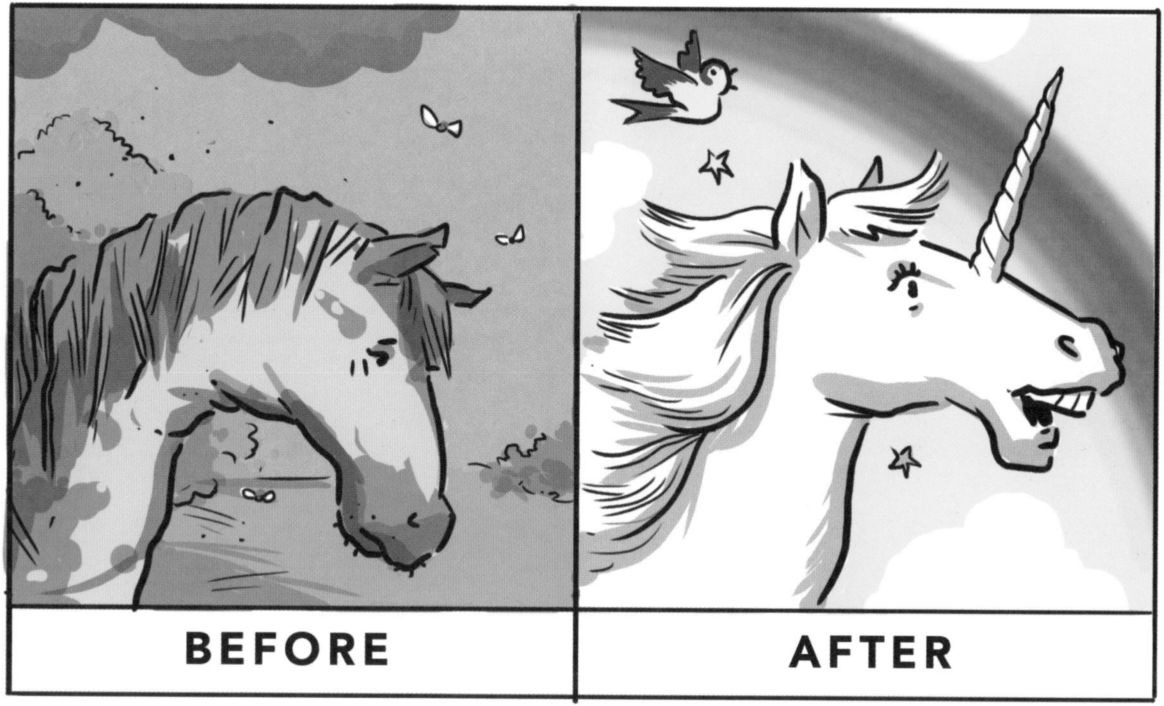
BEFORE
AFTER

#68: Flagpole

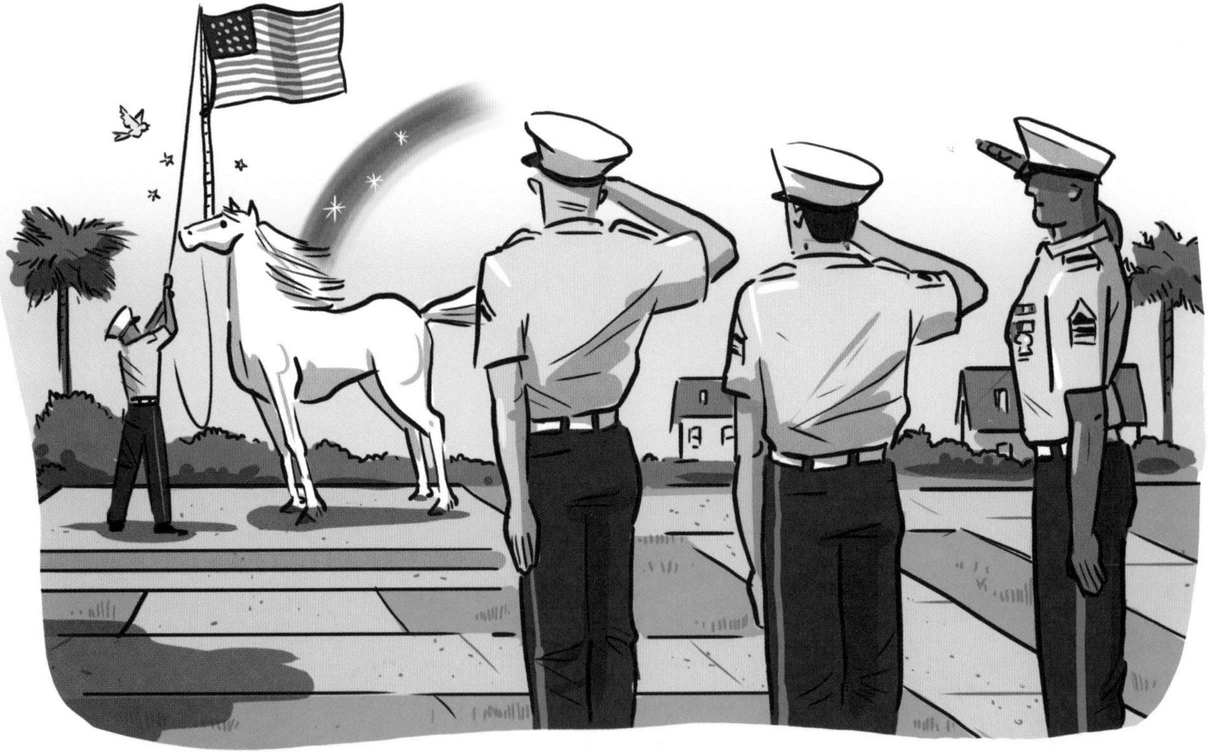

#69: Camping

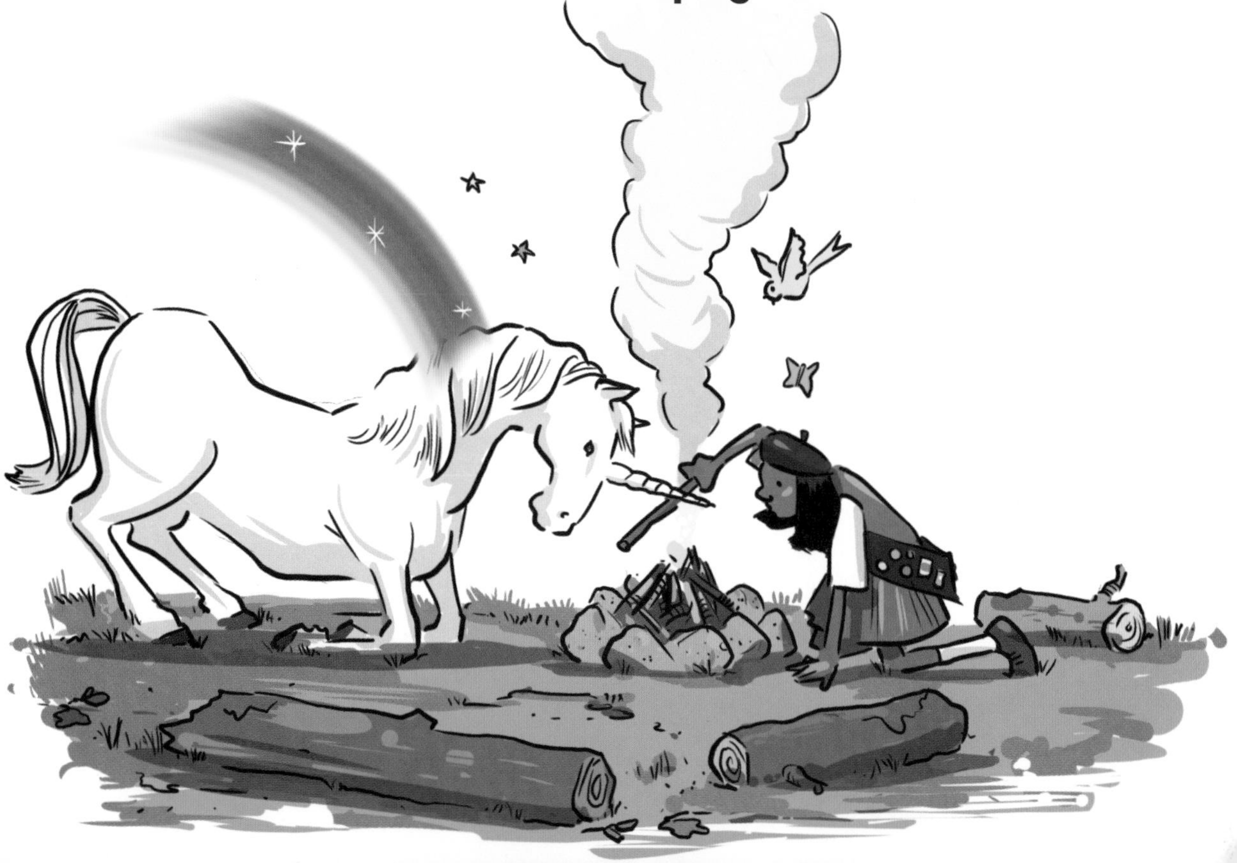

#70: Ring Toss

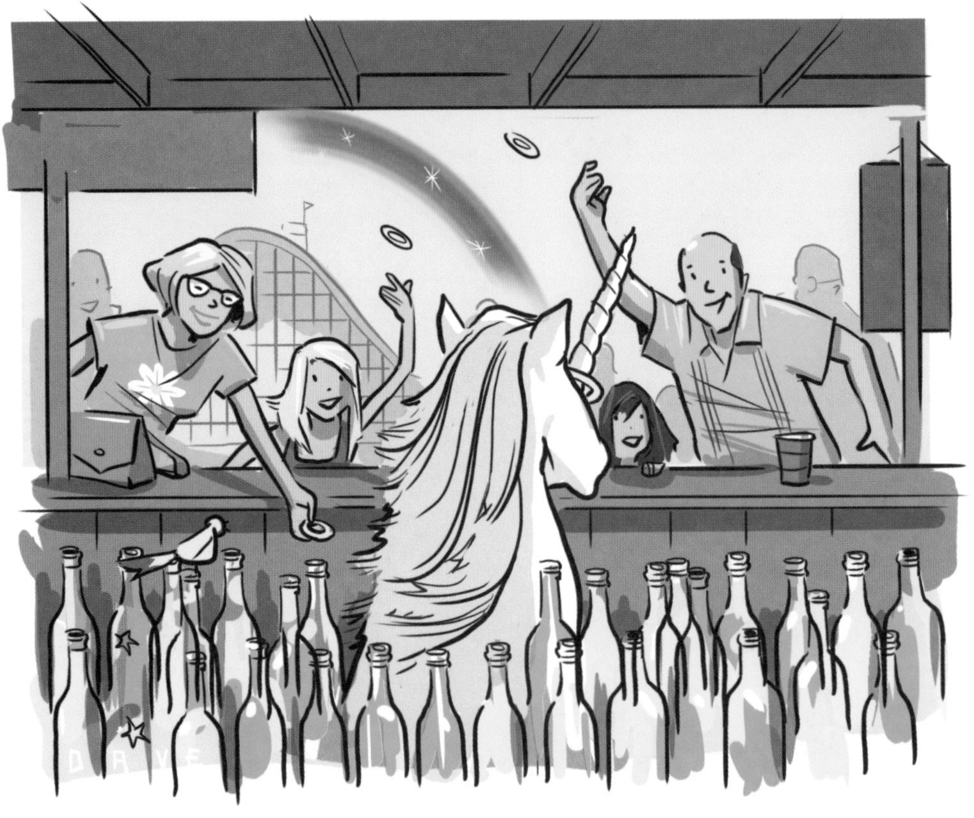

#71: Record Player

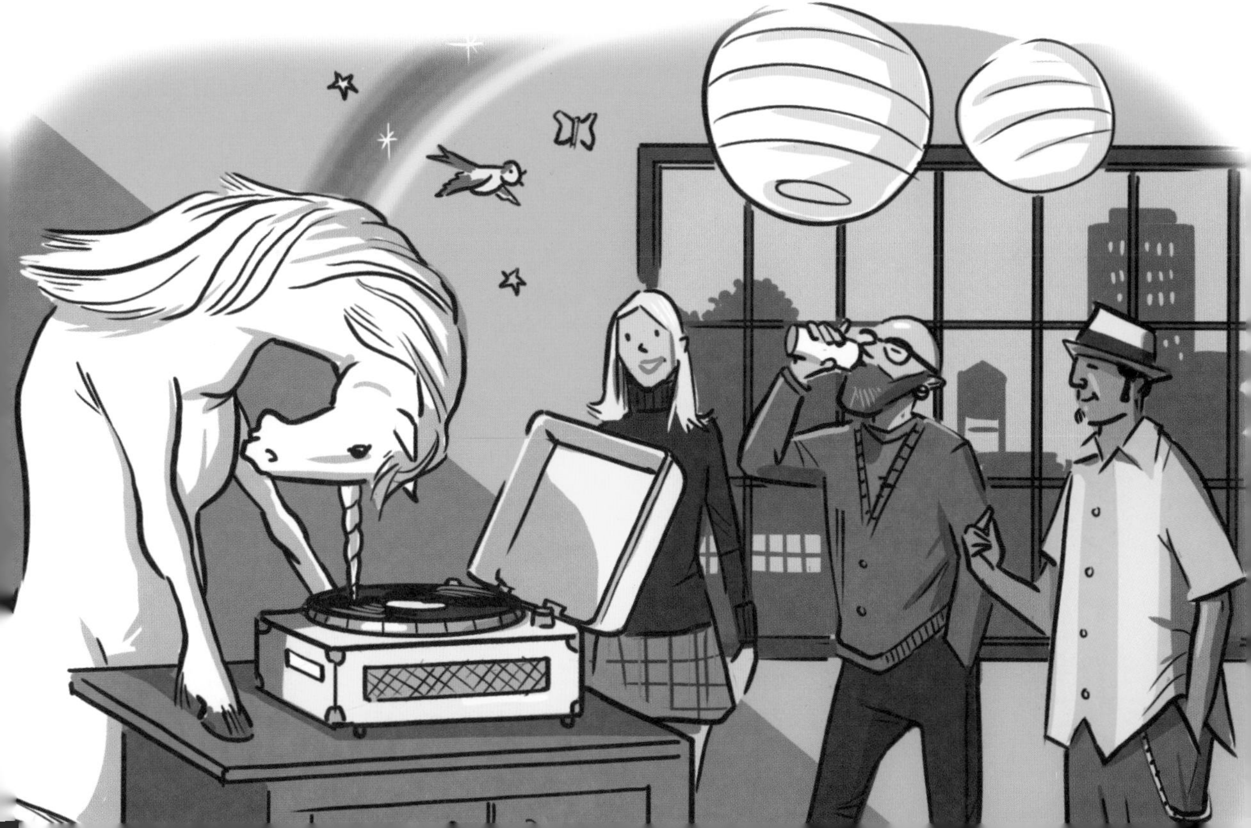

#72: Bell Ringer

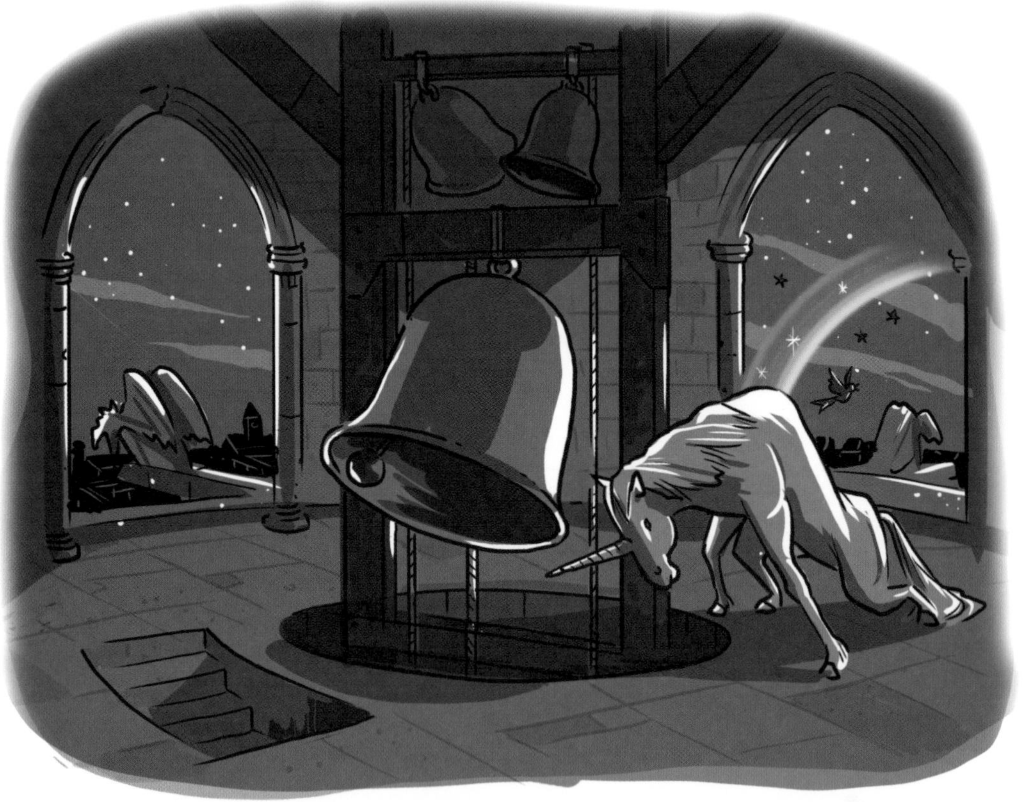

#73: Bell Ringer

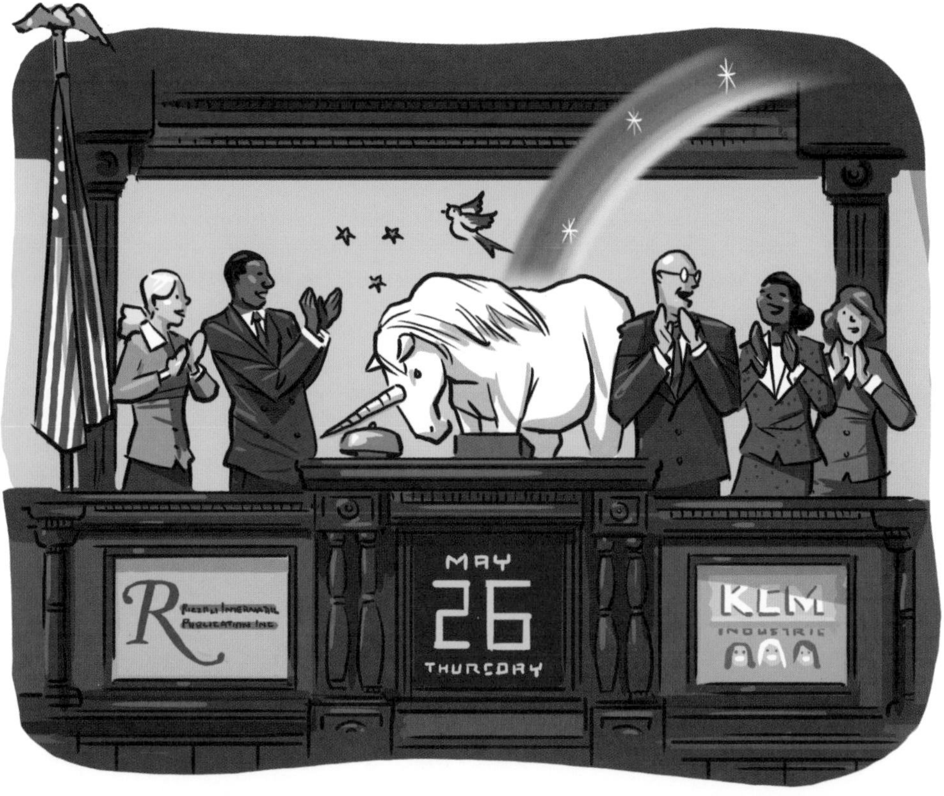
R
MAY
26
THURSDAY
KCM
INDUSTRIE

#74: Windshield Wiper

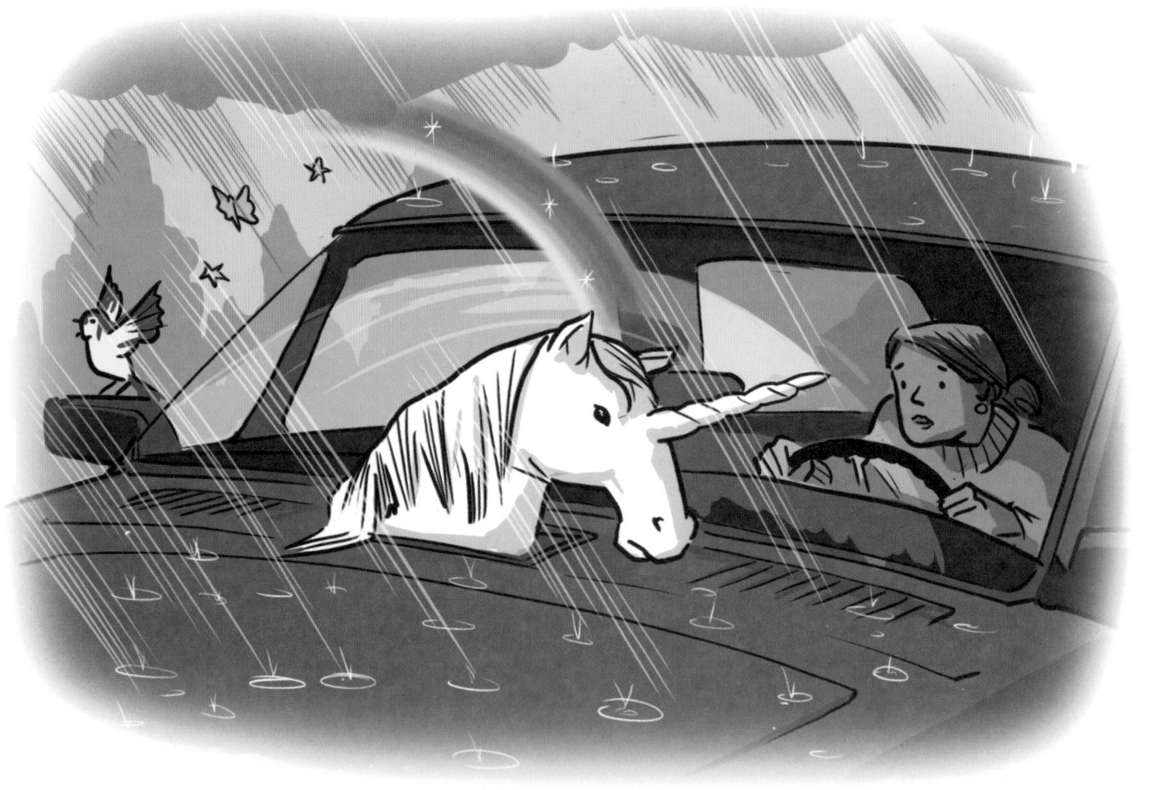

#75: Lightning Rod

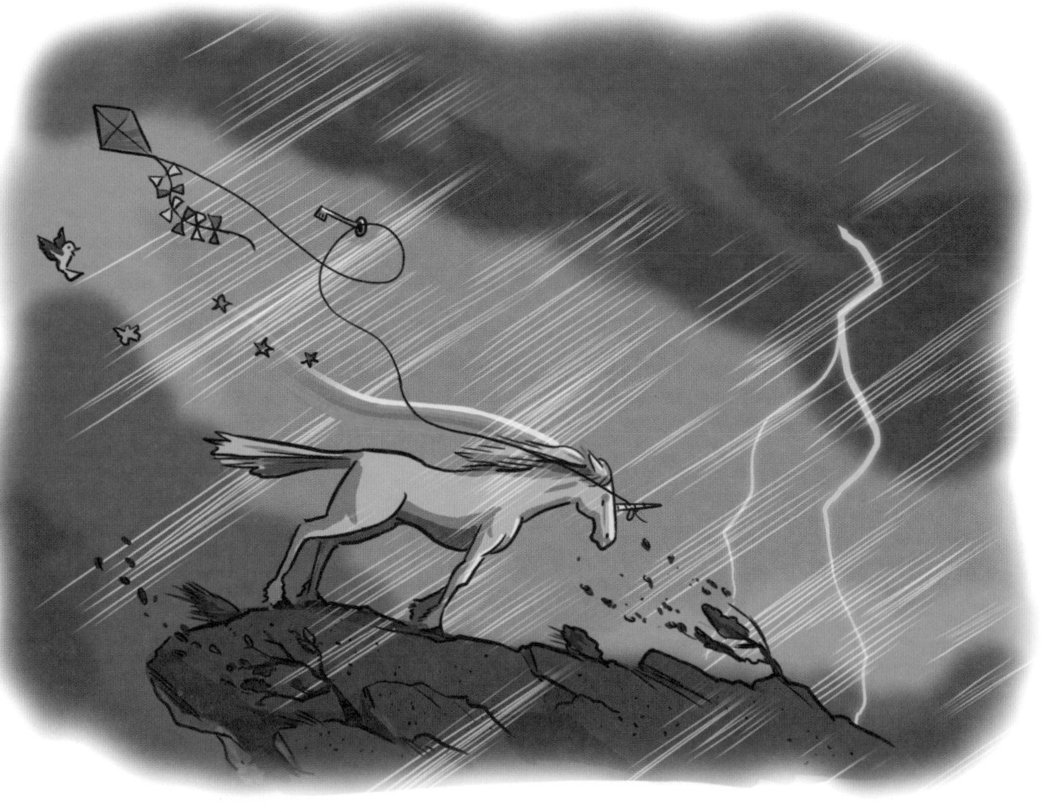

#76: Crafting Tool

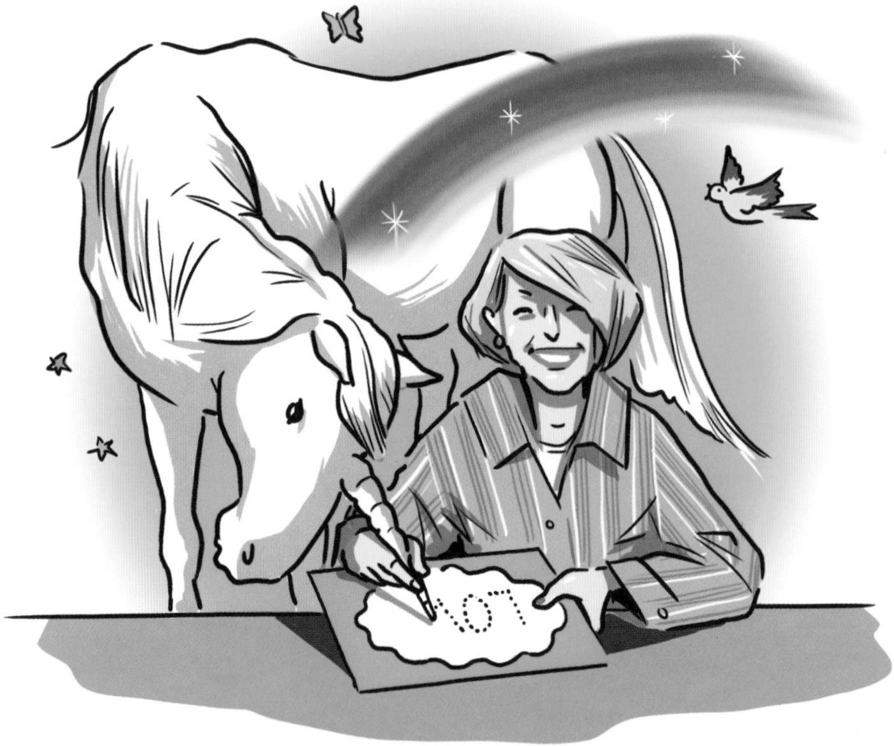
LOL

#77: Easel

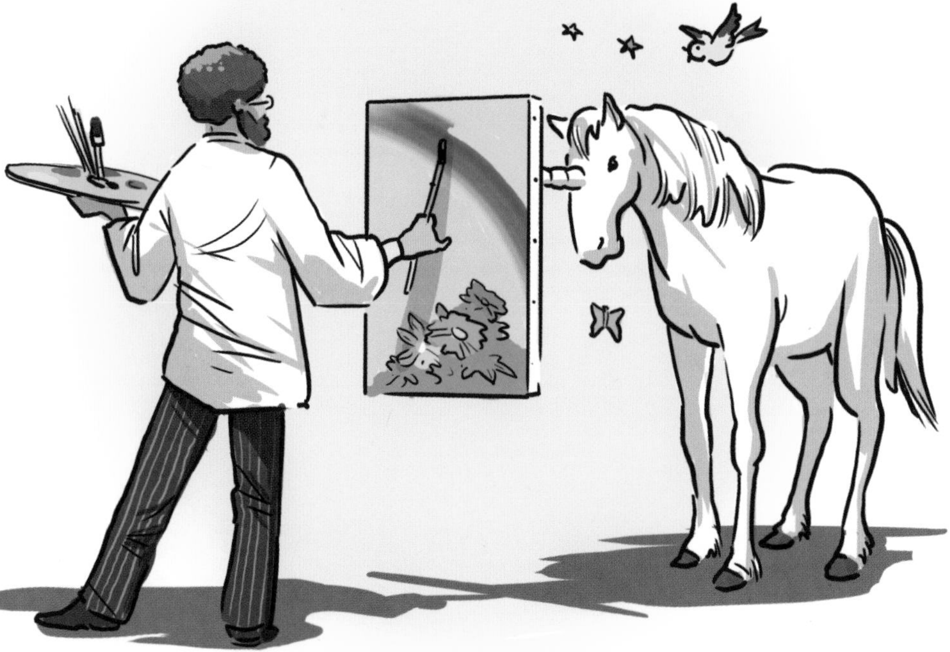

#78: Fishing Spear

#79: Bottle Opener

#80: Dyke Plug

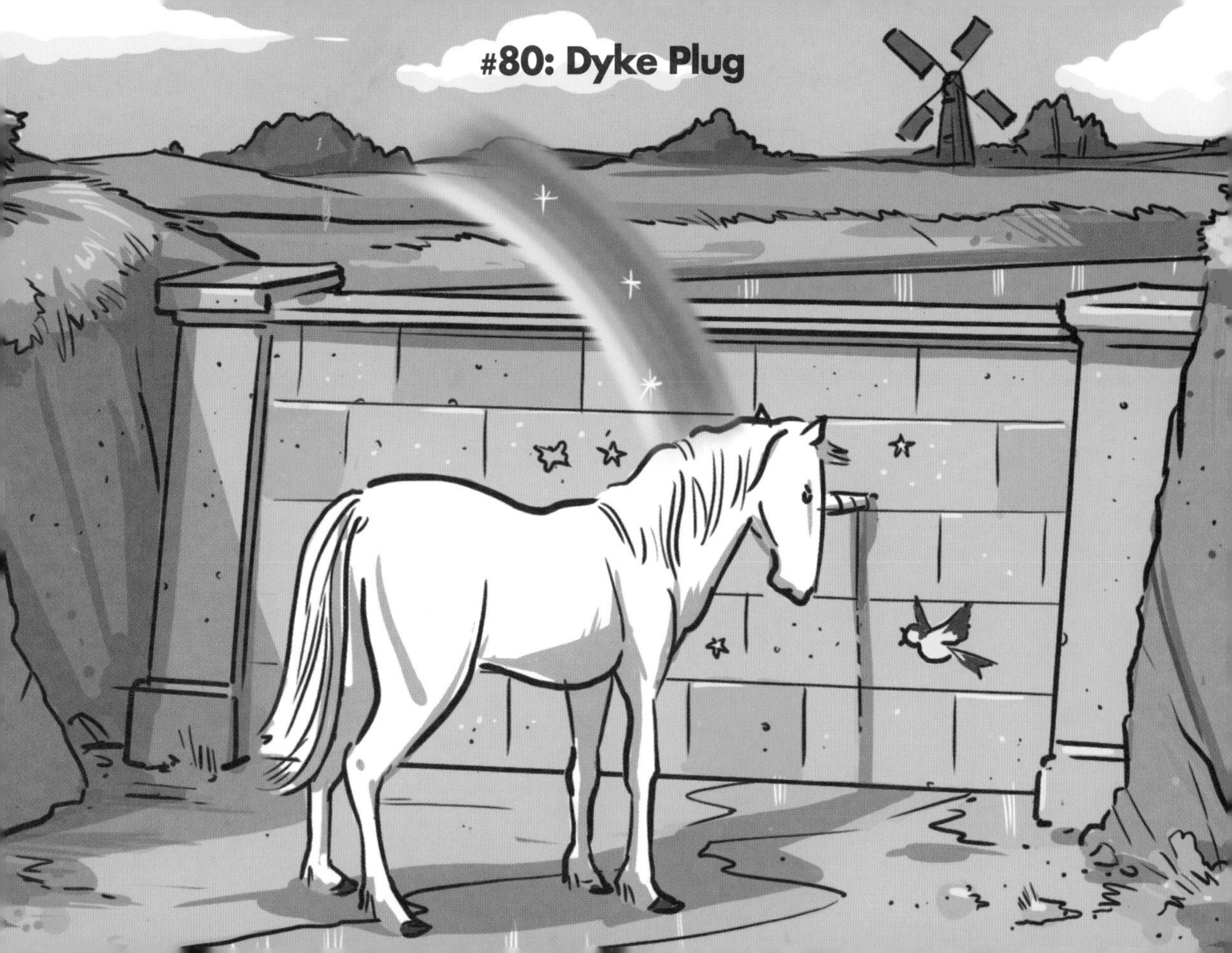

#81: Excuse

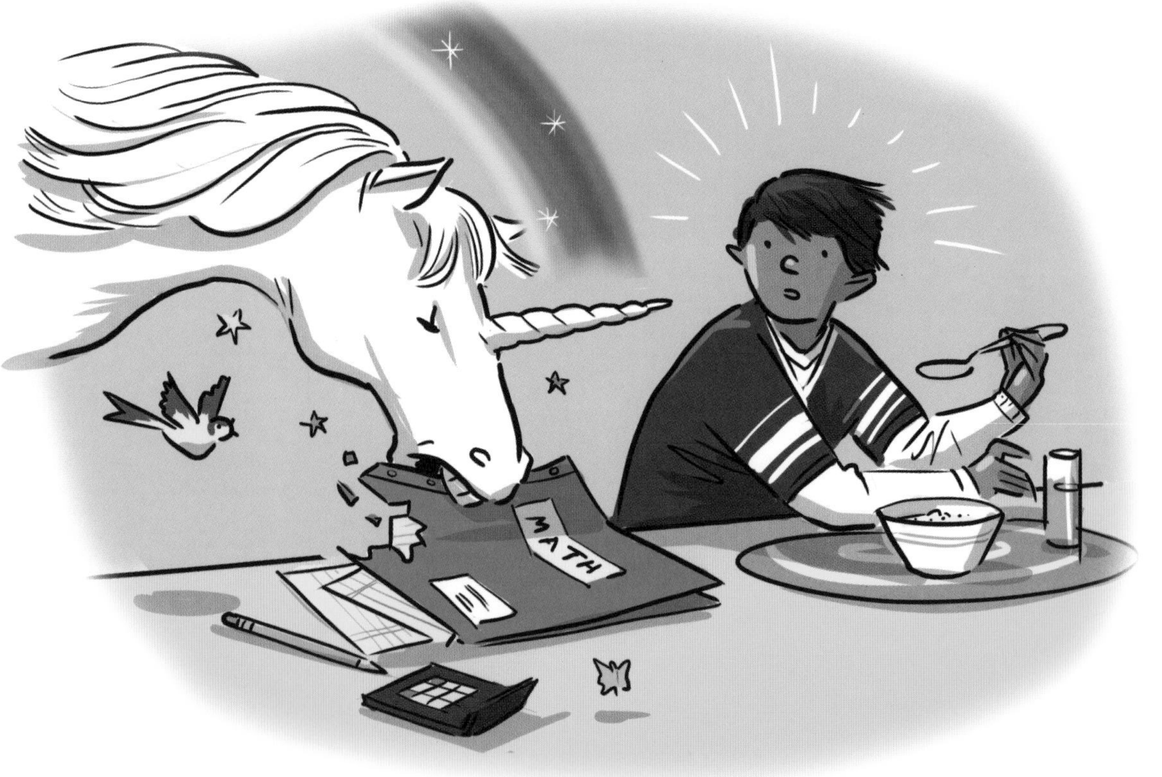
MATH

#82: Q-tip®

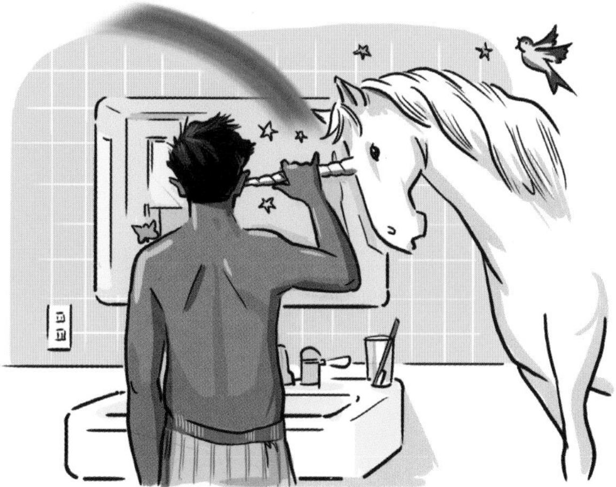

#83: Garnish

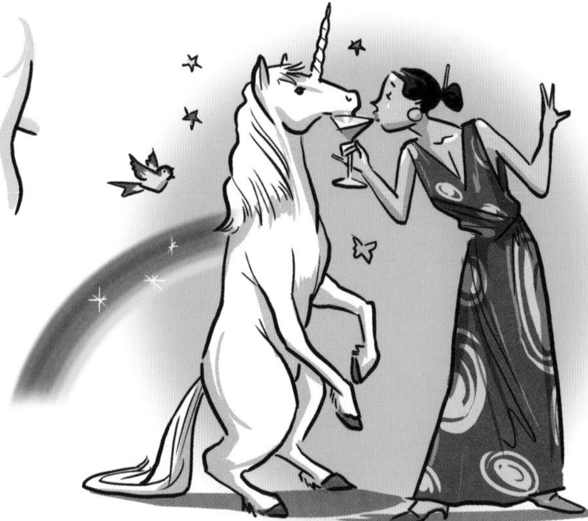

#84: Fourth for Bridge

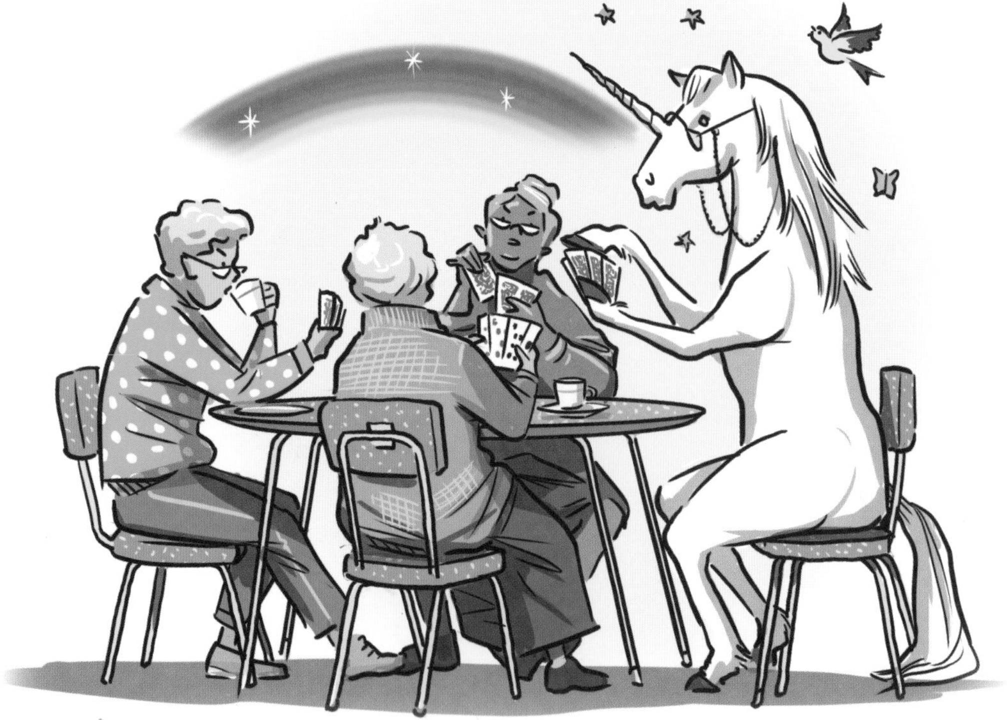

#85: Joystick

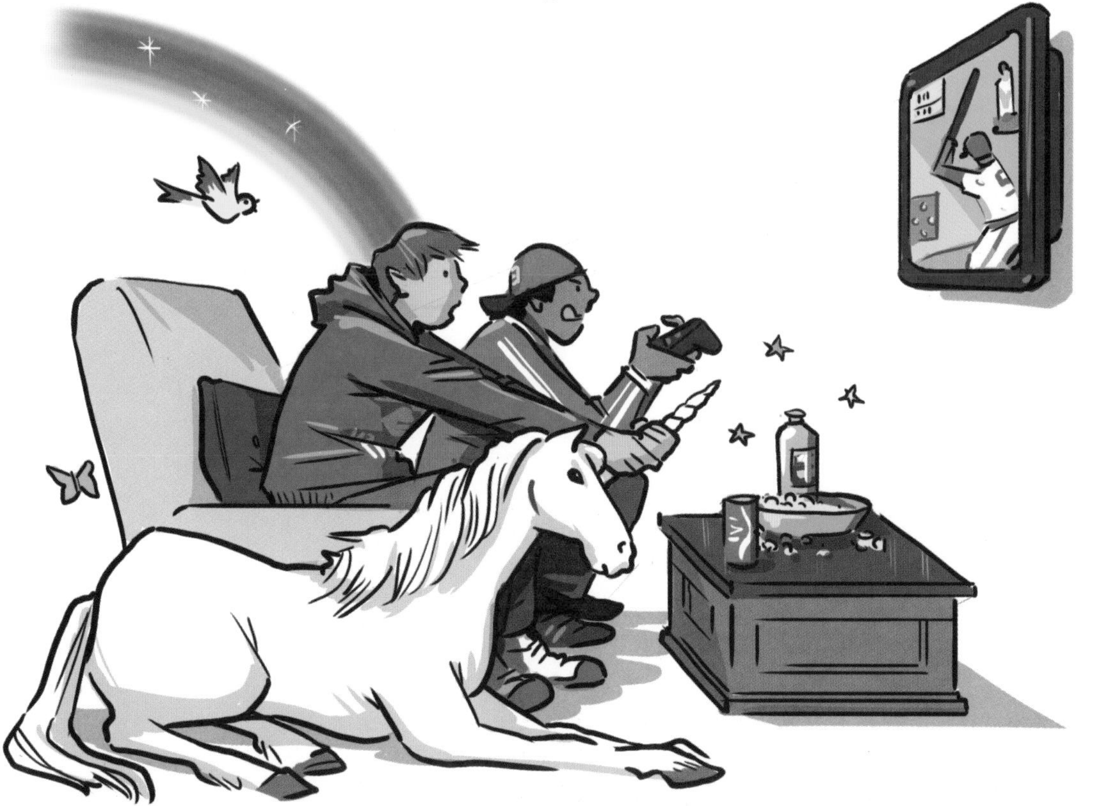

#86: Jan

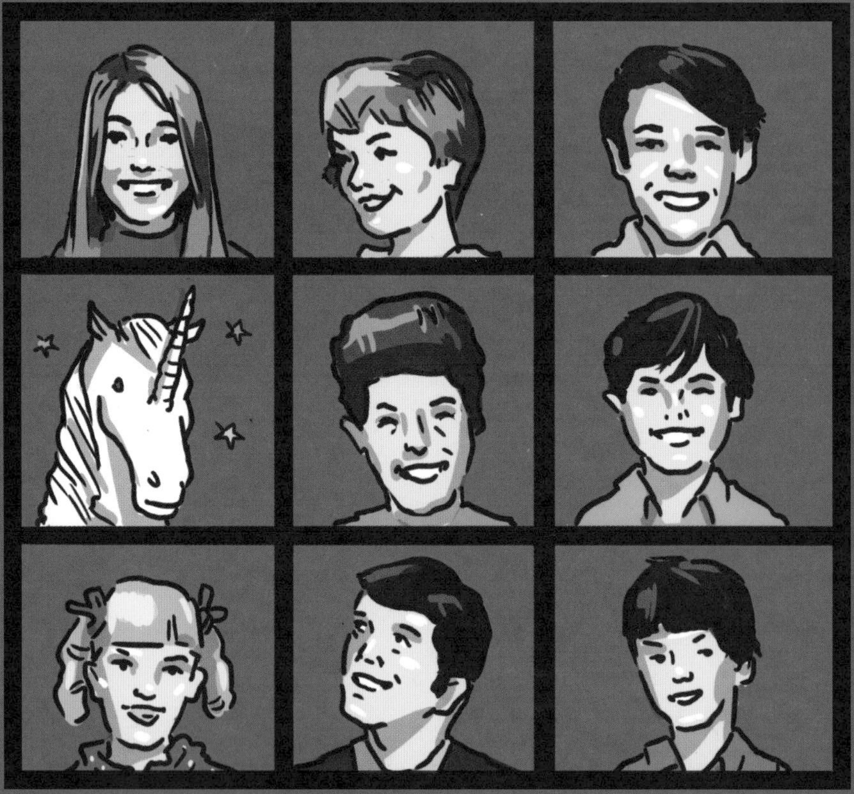

#87: Sigil

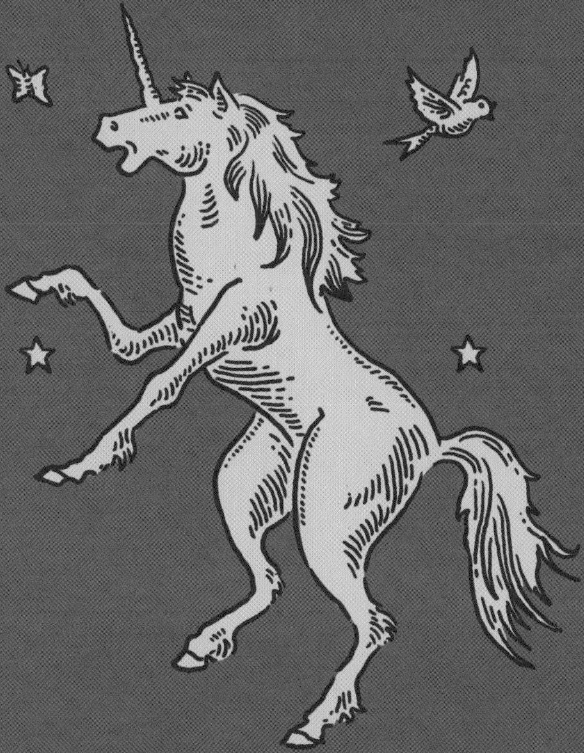

101
USES

#88: Good Cop

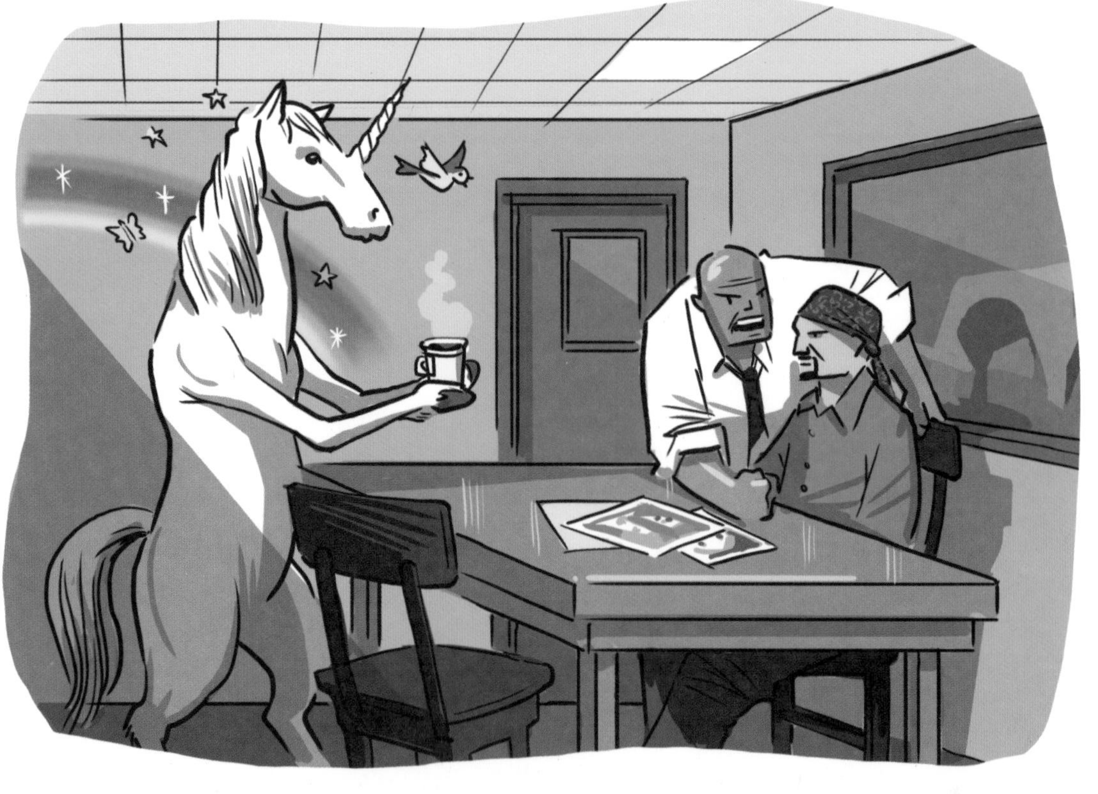

#89: Extra

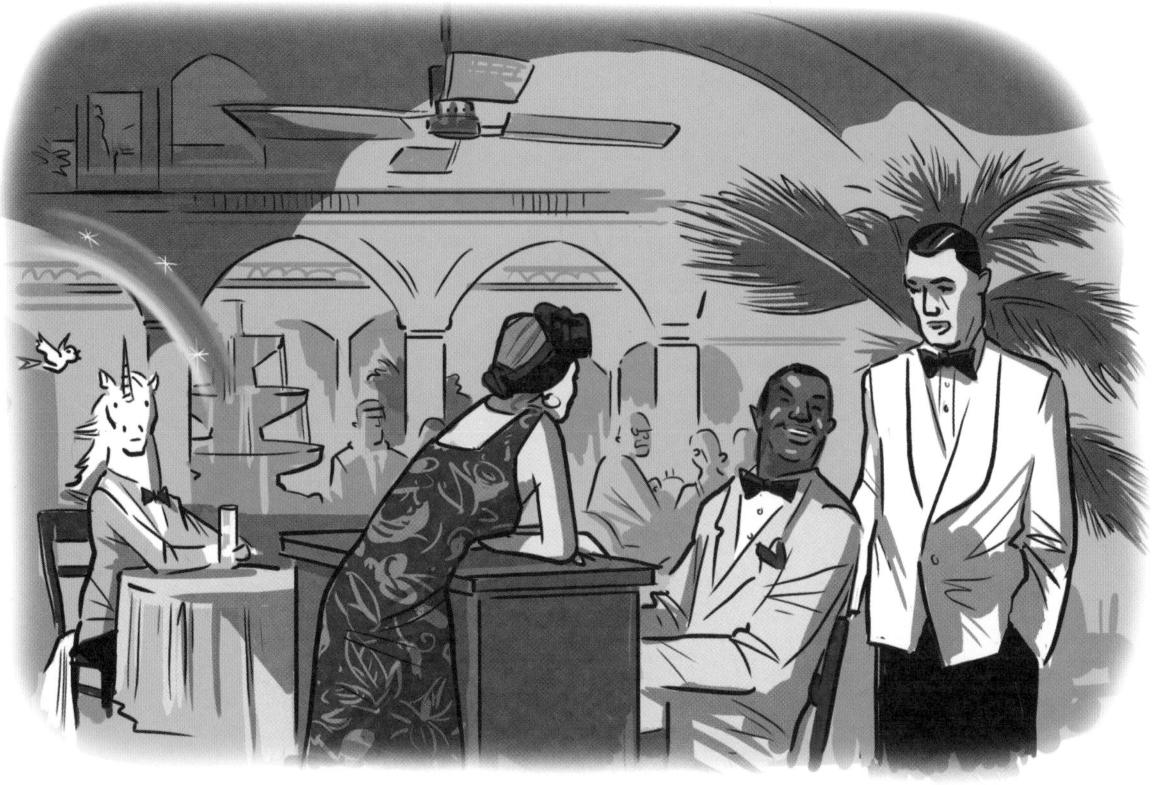

#90: Shining

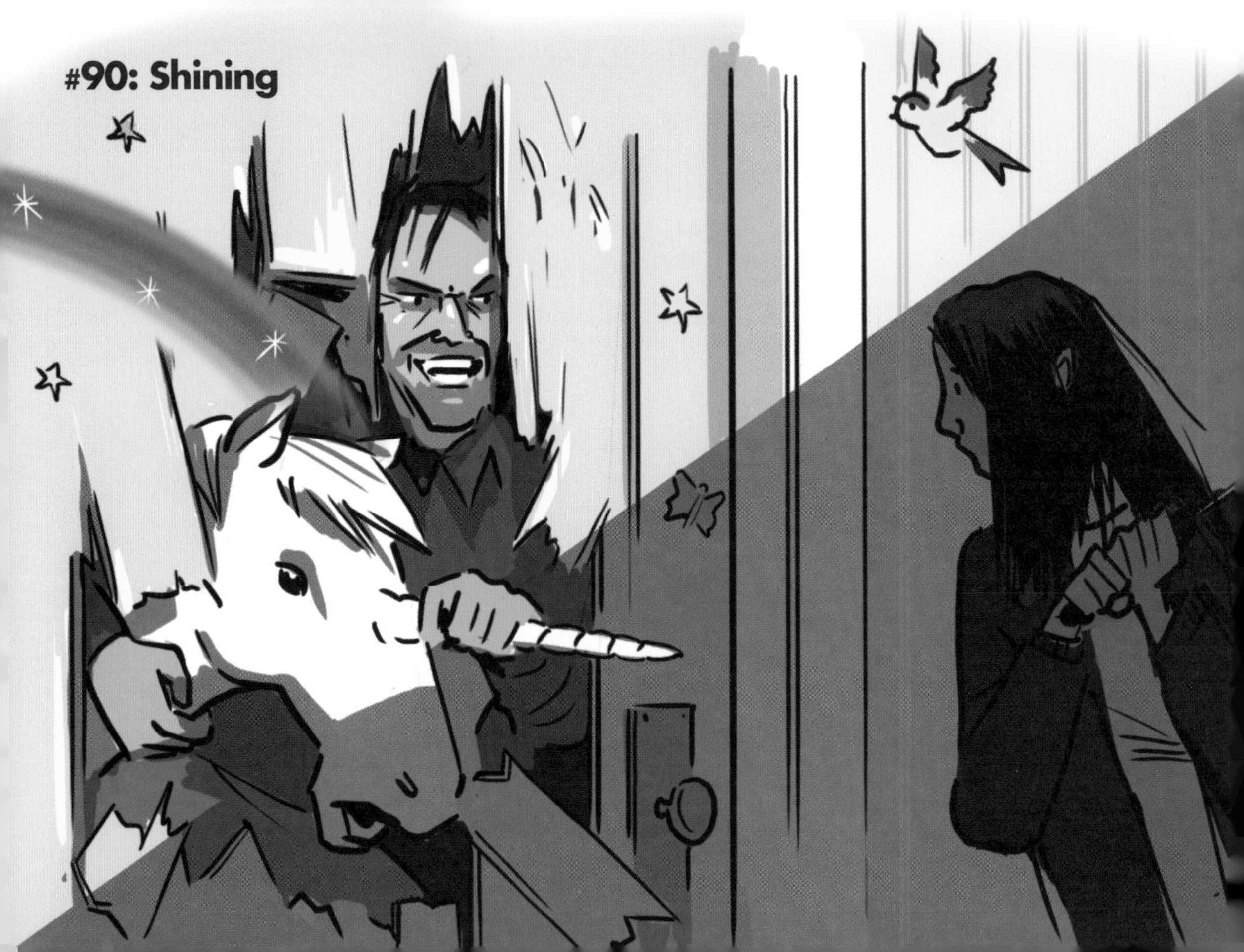

#91: Zombie Killer

#92: Demigod Transport

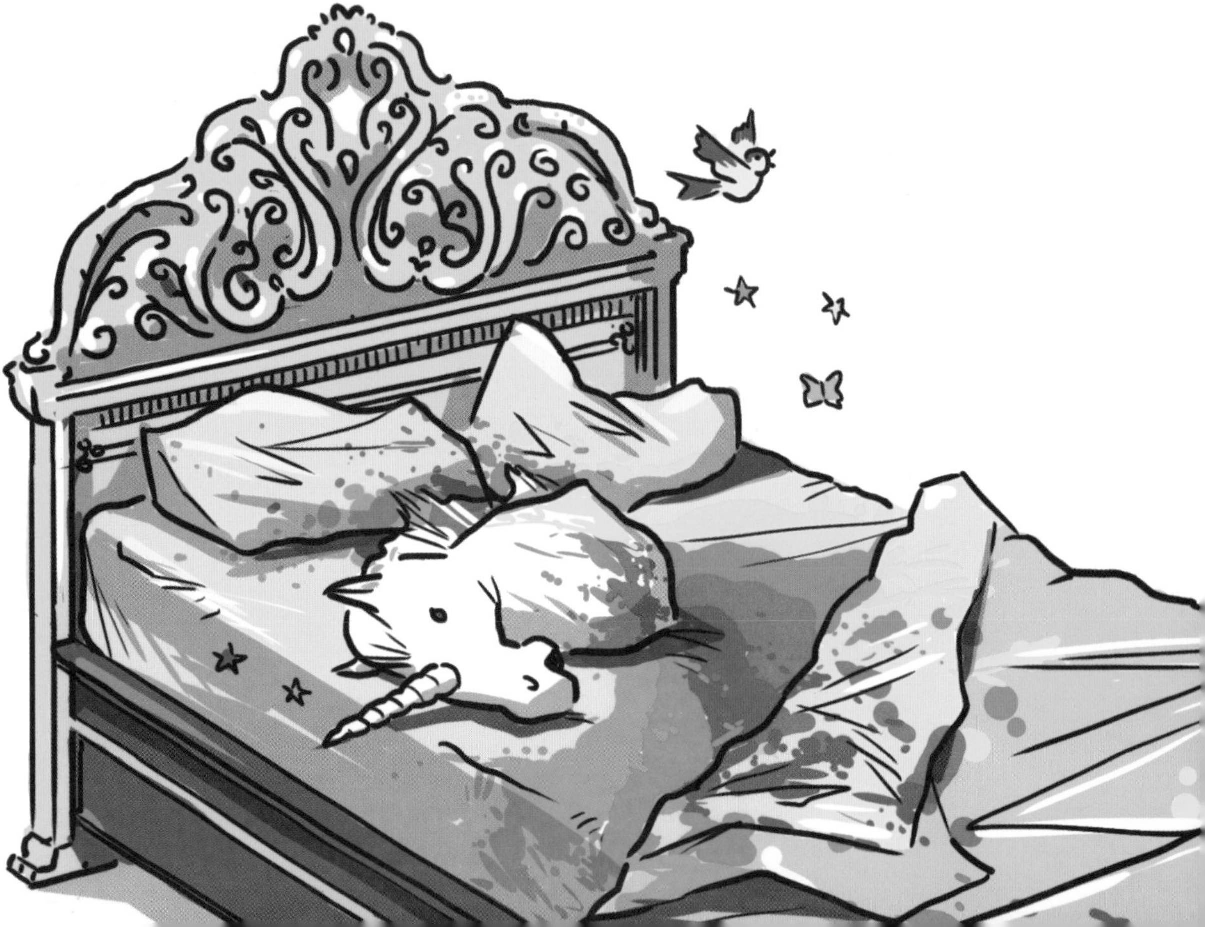

#93: Warning

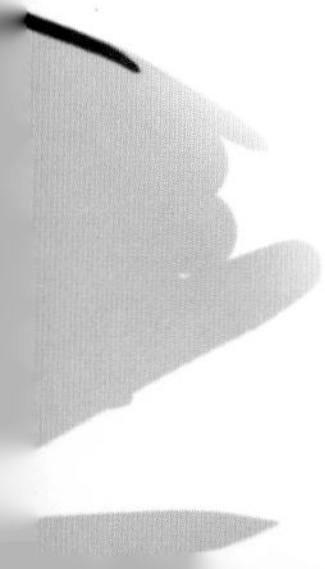

#94: Clothesline

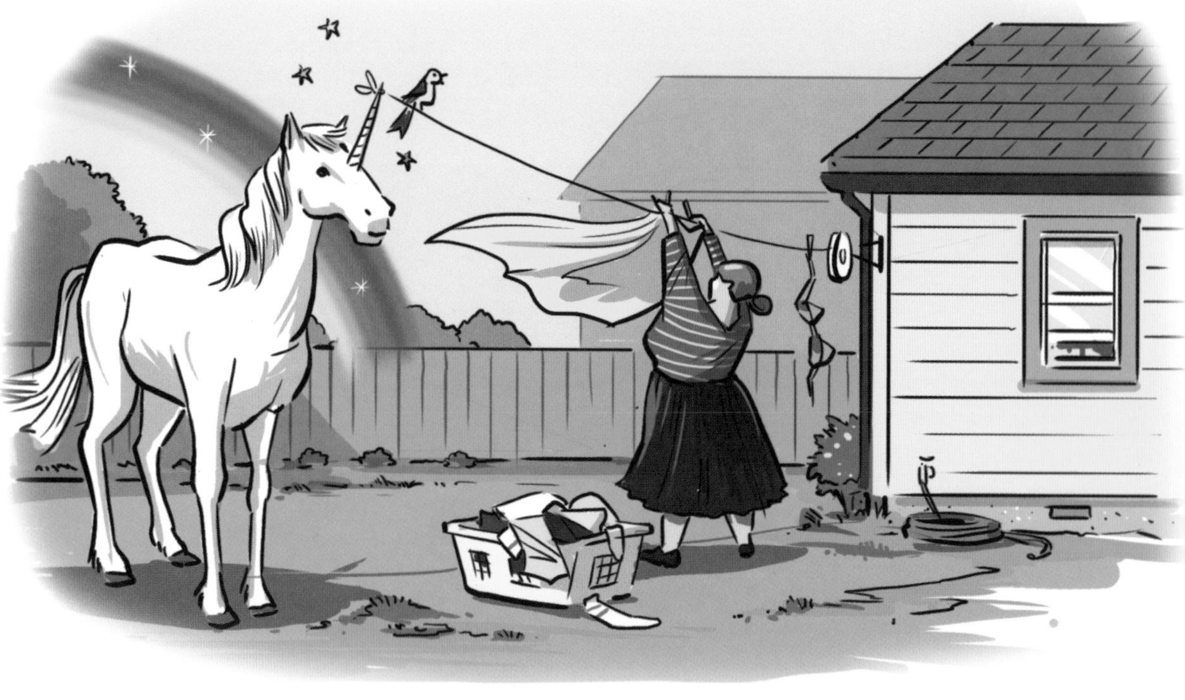

#95: Weather Vane

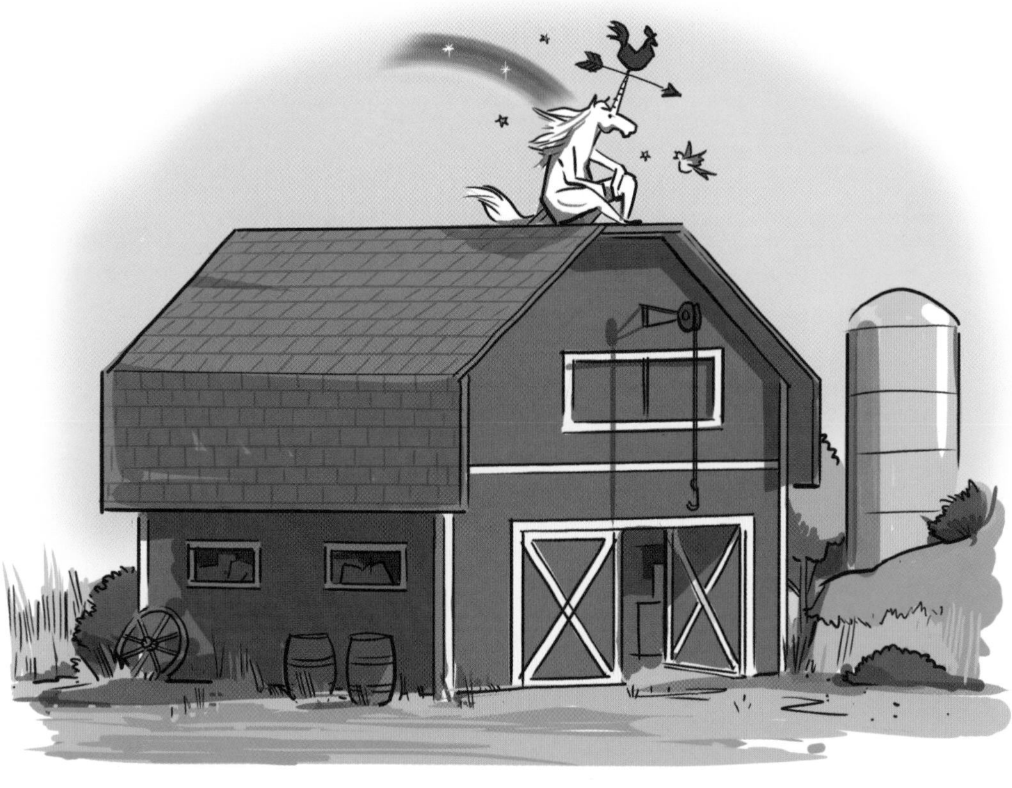

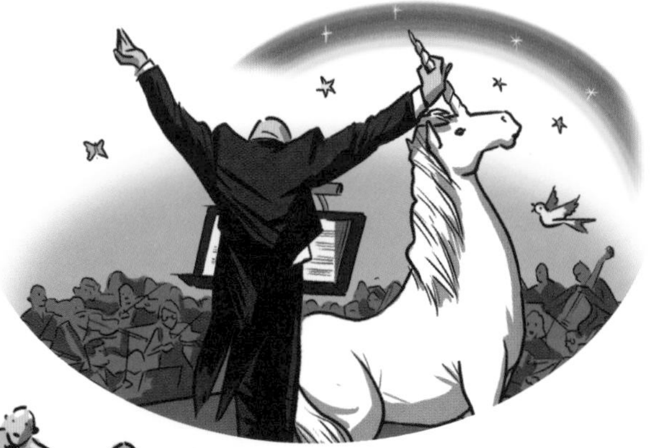

#97: Baton

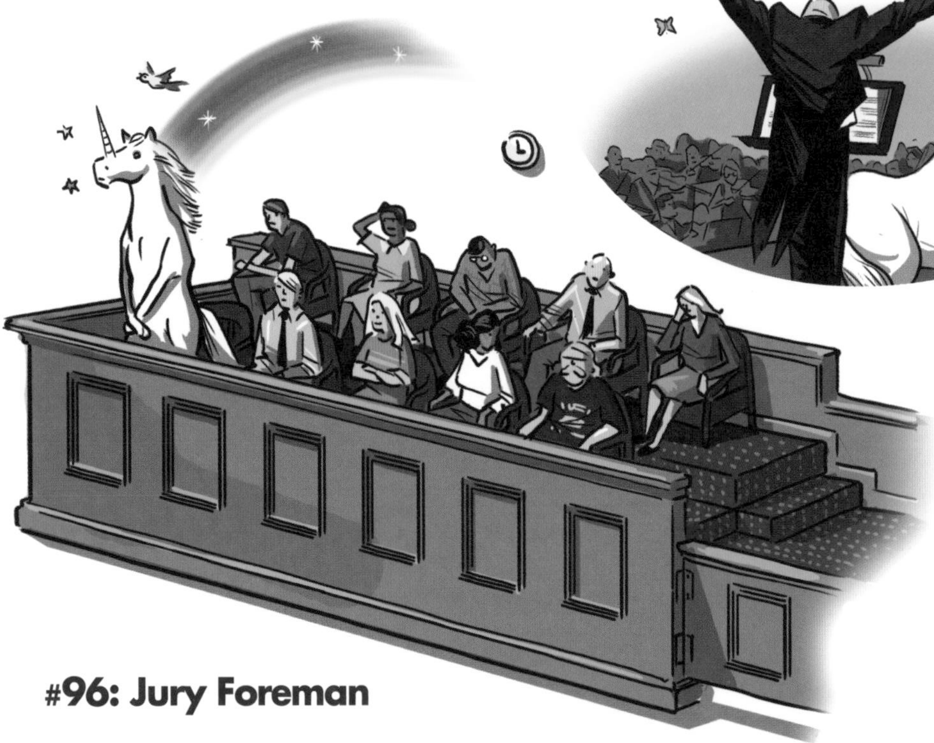

#96: Jury Foreman

#98: Frother

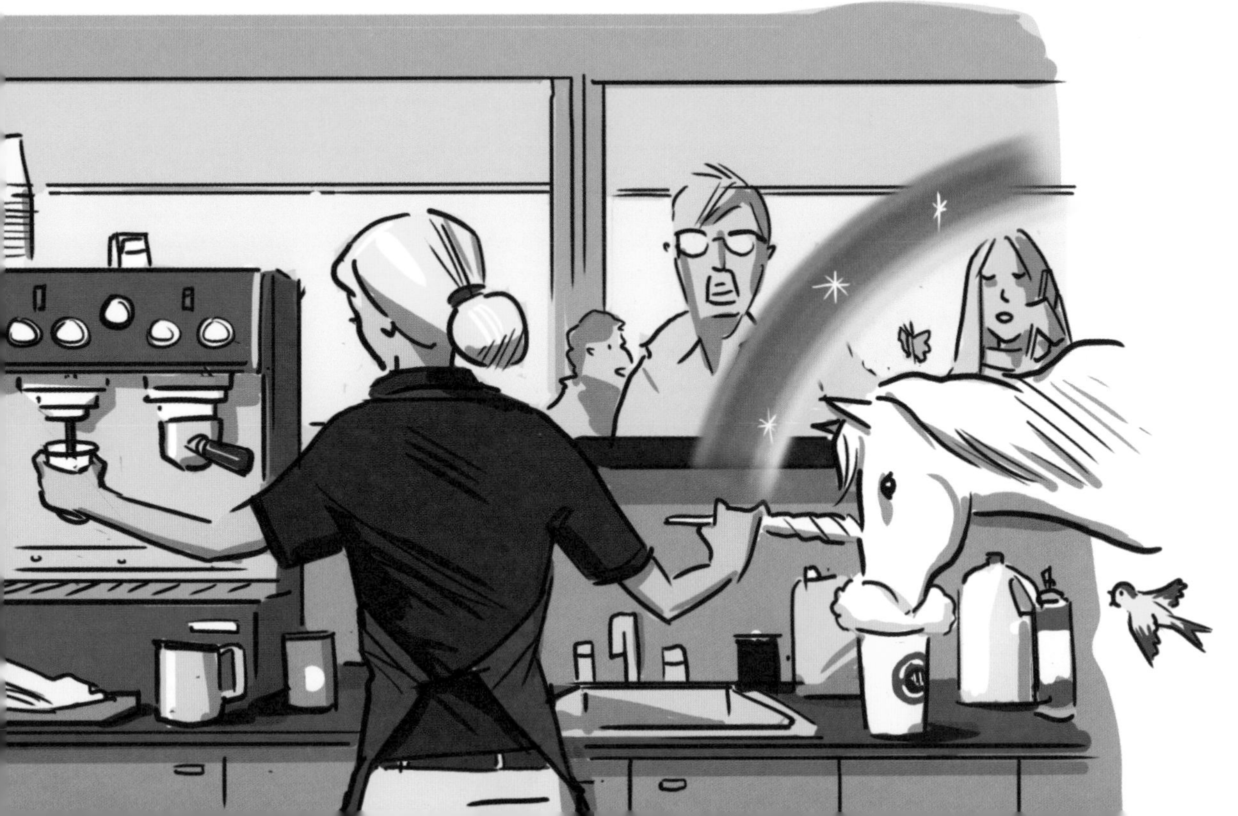

#99: Bridal Party

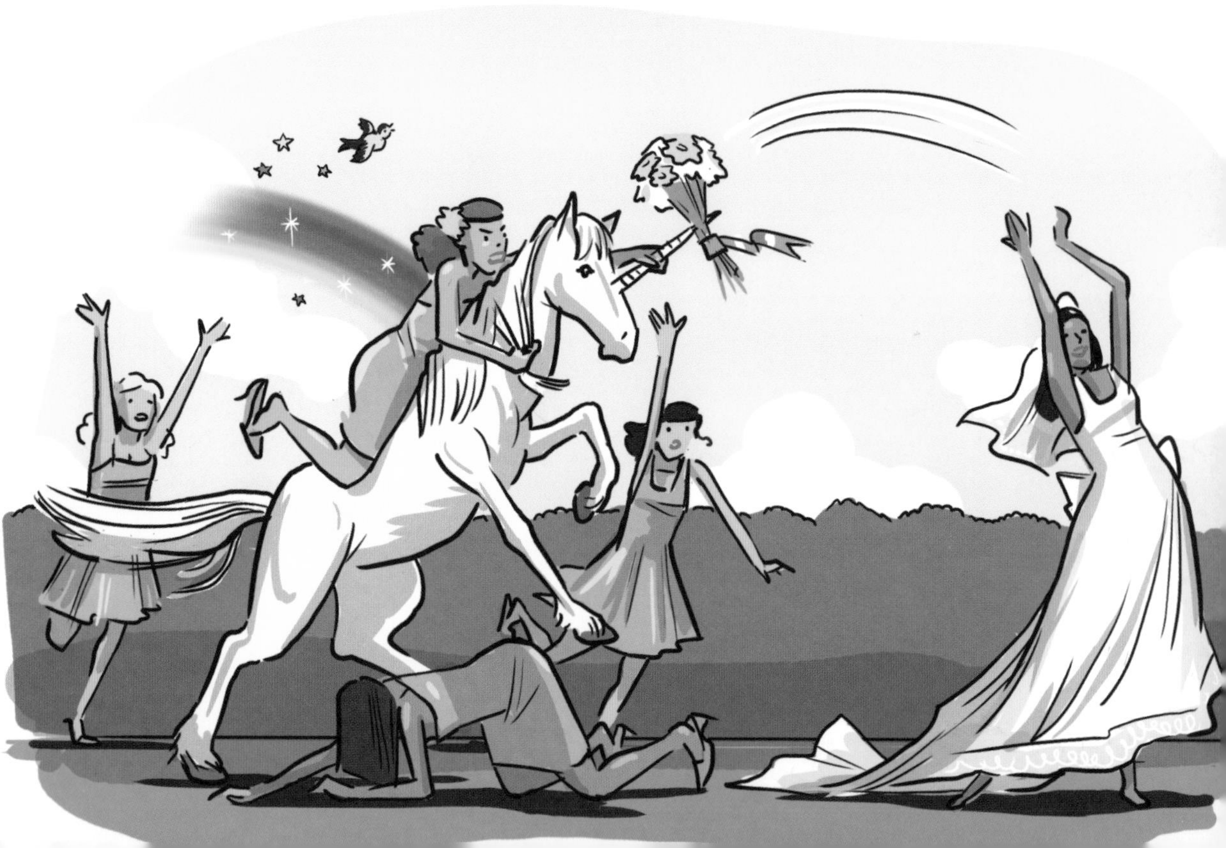

#100: Conversation Starter

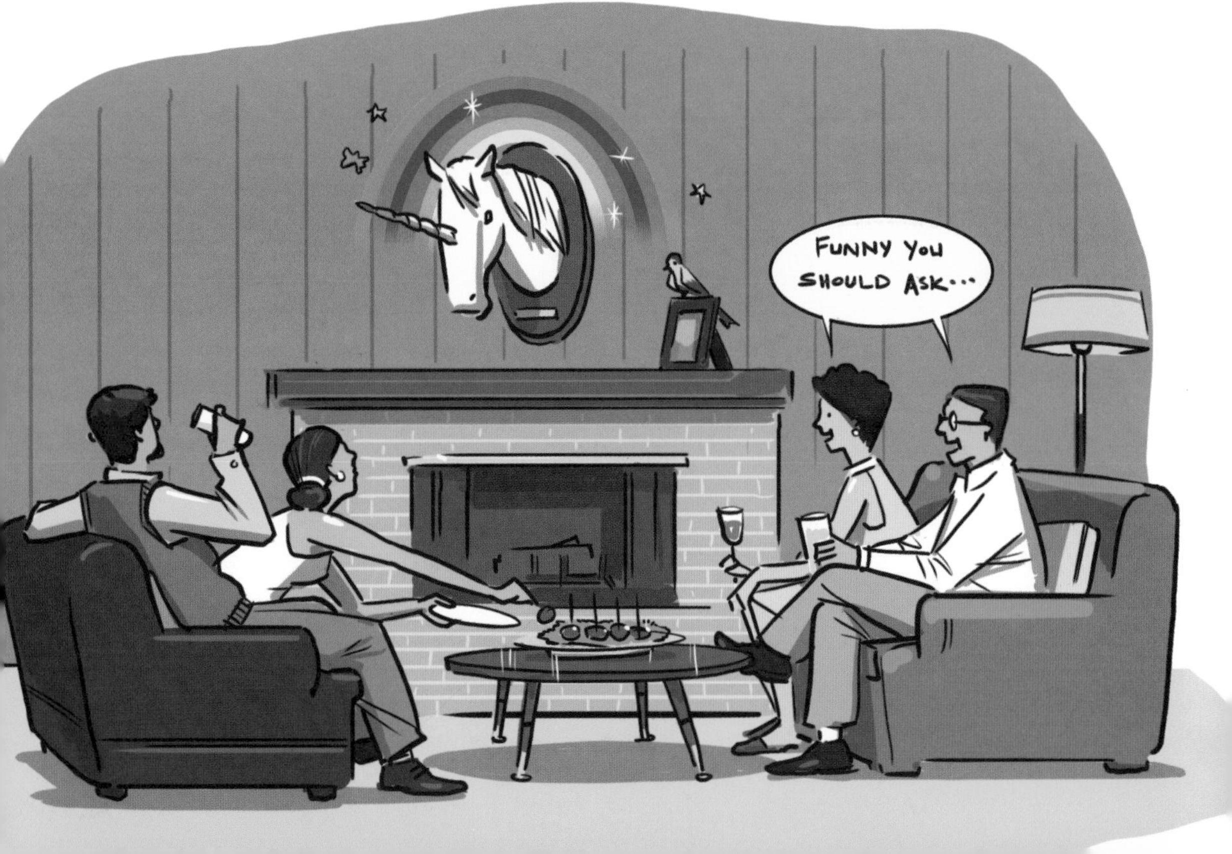
FUNNY YOU SHOULD ASK...

#101: Fountain Pen

Published by Universe Publishing, a division of Rizzoli International Publications, Inc.
300 Park Avenue South • New York, NY 10010 • www.rizzoliusa.com

© 2015 Robb Pearlman • Illustrations © 2015 Dave Urban

2015 2016 2017 2018 2019 / 10 9 8 7 6 5 4 3 2 1

Design: Kayleigh Jankowski • Editor: Jessica Fuller
Printed in China • ISBN-13: 978-0-7893-2910-3 • Library of Congress Catalog Control Number: 2014914585